Praise for *Return on Integrity*

"DON'T READ THIS BOOK unless you want to trade the impotence of superficial leadership for something far more powerful. John Blumberg brilliantly unpacks what we've discovered about extraordinary leaders: They possess a powerful blend of confident humility. Defined by deep-seated core values, passionately lived out loud, one person and one company at a time, they are making a profit while making a difference. Dig deep, and find out how ROI can enrich your life, increase your impact, and equip you to leave a legacy worth remembering."

—**Kevin Freiberg,** Coauthor of the international best seller
NUTS! Southwest Airlines' Crazy Recipe for Business and Personal Success

"Your life complexity is magnified by the enterprise you lead. You will face inevitable blitzes. Are you ready to step up and face each blitz? The courageous path John Blumberg calls you to travel will fuel your ability to turn trials into triumphs and steward relationships for shared joy!"

—**Jeff Kemp,** author of *Facing The Blitz,* former
NFL quarterback and VP at Family Life Today

"Great title . . . We must return to integrity—personally and professionally! Great book to encourage going deep into the company culture, the employees, and your core values, which determine the success of your enterprise every single time!"

—**Naomi Rhode,** CSP, CPAE Speaker Hall of Fame,
cofounder SmartPractice

"One might assume that faith-based organizations have clearly stated values and lead from their core. But leaders of these communities are not immune to 'the drift.' *Return on Integrity* is an incredible wake-up call to all leaders as we take a deep look within and begin to lead from the most important and effective place: our core! John Blumberg provides powerful leadership insight and practical application that will empower any senior pastor, not-for-profit president, or CEO to be true to themselves and more successful at accomplishing their mission."

—**Shawn Williams,** executive pastor of leadership development
at the Central Christian Church, Las Vegas

"In your hands, you hold a force for good. Never before has the need for a message of conduct, standards, accountability, and integrity been in higher demand. This book will change lives and impact decisions in all walks of life and business. Read it. Live it. Share it. Once in a blue moon, a change-the-world book is published. And, now you have it."

—**Mark LeBlanc,** author of *Never Be the Same* and *Growing Your Business*

"John Blumberg has given us a priceless gift with this engaging book. Integrity and values are at the top of the list of the important and timely topics in individual lives and organizational cultures. As a psychologist for over three decades, I have worked with literally thousands who, tragically, have not heeded the principles, the *why-tos*, and the *how-tos* John has described so well. I've walked through the rubble of their lives with them after what began as a slight drift from values either gradually or suddenly morphed into a devastating derailment. The identification of and adherence to what really matters are hallmarks of the healthy personality, of personal well-being, of whole relationships, and of long-term career success. This is a book that I will recommend and 'assign' over and over!"

—**Dr. Bev Smallwood,** psychologist and
author of *This Wasn't Supposed to Happen to Me*

ROI

Return On Integrity

The New Definition of ROI
and Why Leaders Need to Know It

JOHN G. BLUMBERG

GREENLEAF
BOOK GROUP PRESS

This publication is designed to provide accurate and authoritative information in regard to the subject matter covered. It is sold with the understanding that the publisher and author are not engaged in rendering legal, accounting, or other professional services. If legal advice or other expert assistance is required, the services of a competent professional should be sought.

Published by Greenleaf Book Group Press
Austin, Texas
www.greenleafbookgroup.com

Scripture taken from *The Message*. Copyright 1993, 1994, 1995, 1996, 2000, 2001, 2002. Used by permission of NavPress Publishing Group.

Distributed by Greenleaf Book Group

For ordering information or special discounts for bulk purchases, please contact Greenleaf Book Group at PO Box 91869, Austin, TX 78709, 512.891.6100.

Design and composition by Greenleaf Book Group
Cover design by Greenleaf Book Group

Cataloging-in-Publication data

ISBN 13: 978-1-62634-262-0

eBook ISBN: 978-1-62634-263-7

Part of the Tree Neutral® program, which offsets the number of trees consumed in the production and printing of this book by taking proactive steps, such as planting trees in direct proportion to the number of trees used: www.treeneutral.com

Printed in the United States of America on acid-free paper

17 18 19 20 21   10 9 8 7 6 5 4 3 2

First Edition

*Dedicated to each and every leader at the top
who desires to lead from the depth of his or her core.*

*I also dedicate this to my most beloved Drift Catchers of all . . .
my wife, Cindy, and our three children: Ryan, Kelly, and Julie.*

Knowing what is right is like deep water in the heart.

A wise person draws from the well within.

Proverbs 20:5

—*The Message*

Contents

Opening Thoughts

This book is a road map. It is less about finding answers and more about finding your way. In fact, one of its greatest benefits will be to raise questions in your head. And, in your role as a leader at the top, it is guaranteed to get you thinking! My hope is that your thinking will lead you to relevant, creative, and credible solutions. By design, this is not a long book. Neither is it a short read. I hope it will keep you thinking in ways you haven't thought before. This book is not as much about getting it right, as it is about doing what is right; I trust that in doing what is right, you will certainly get more right.

This book is not about strength, but it is about courage. It is not about how you appear, but it is about who you really are. It is not about getting rich. This book is about being rich. It is not about stretching for your highest goals; it is more about digging for your deepest treasures. It is not about saving capitalism, but it is about redeeming it. I am less interested in you being wowed by new ideas, and more interested in you seeing old ideas in powerful new ways. This book is not about leadership development. It is about the kind of development that should matter most to leaders. It is about strengthening your core and the qualities of leadership that will emerge when you do.

Anyone who knows me, or who has seen me speak, knows about my love of stories and the critical role they play in bringing content to life. Here, however, I'm not going to give you a plethora of success stories about other leaders. Leaders don't need those stories. They develop them. This book is about you becoming a leader who actually creates your own stories—stories where followers find precisely what they need.

Let's be clear from the beginning. This book may be the most important book on business strategy you may ever read. You may not immediately recognize the source of this strategy, because for far too long we have ignored it. But when it comes to leading, this strategy isn't just one more thing. It is everything.

The ROI of this book will not come from the book you are holding in your hands. It will come from within you. The ROI you will realize depends solely on whether you have the guts to truly lead. I fully trust that you do—or that someone thinks you do—otherwise you wouldn't be reading this book right now. So let's get started.

It will be more of an adventure than you ever dreamed!

In the Spruce Plot
At the Morton Arboretum
Lisle, Illinois

Overview

I was sitting at the foot of the bed, in a downtown Denver hotel, watching CNN. It was about 5:30 PM on a cloudy Thursday—March 14, 2002. I had just come from speaking with a training room full of Arthur Andersen employees from the Denver office. I had been speaking in the Los Angeles office just two days prior.

While I had left a wonderful eighteen-year career at the firm just five years before, I was coming home to talk with a family I loved—in their darkest hour. As I sat on the end of the bed, CNN was reporting that the Department of Justice had, in fact, just announced the indictment of Arthur Andersen as a firm rather than indicting individuals involved directly in the Enron situation. It would prove to be a decisive nail in the coffin for the firm, affecting the careers of its 85,000 professionals and their families worldwide.

It's hard to describe how hard and how personal that news hit.

As I sat there trying to process the reality of the news and its impact, I simply said, "Dear God, if we can all learn something from any of this, then it will be worth it. But please let us learn something." The key word was *all*, because I was certain that this lesson wasn't something that just the people of Arthur Andersen or even the people of Enron needed to learn. It was all of us!

That question was *What's the lesson in this?* Maybe, more importantly, *What is the solution?*

Sitting at the foot of that bed was a defining moment for me, though I didn't realize it at the time. It was hard that night to see anything but darkness. It is only in looking back that I understand how that prayer would not let go of me.

Sometimes lessons come slowly. At least the really important ones. I can still picture sitting at the foot of that bed. Nothing changed that night. It would, however, be the first step in a journey that would eventually clarify everything.

As that clarity came into focus, it raised some important questions.

What if you got to the end of your career and realized you had missed something that could have totally defined your leadership, your success, and ultimately your legacy? What if you realized you had dismissed a powerful tool and an authentic strategy that you always had right at your fingertips? Or, more precisely, right at your core?

As a fiscally minded executive, you might be especially disappointed to know that employing this tool would have cost you very little in comparison to the potential it could have delivered. It might have saved you millions. For certain executives, it could have saved them everything.

Some executives discount it. Others ignore it. Some have manipulated it for their own gain. But only a few have intentionally led with it.

Many executives have embraced the tip of the iceberg of this strategy and then checked it off their list as if it were something that could be completed rather than lived. Still others have been comfortable with it at the organizational level, but found themselves unable to take it to the personal level.

Some executives have thought it was just all about the soft stuff, when in truth it was just too hard for them to do. Many were seduced by the momentum of the time, and some weren't strong enough to embrace what they mistakenly wrote off as an approach for the weak.

Many executives drift, while some of their colleagues actually drown. Few executives live up to their enormous potential; and because of their negligence, they let their followers down. They don't do it on purpose. But the consequences are just the same. Ignoring the truth doesn't change the truth. But ignoring the truth changes us.

We will never truly know the cost of the lost opportunities. That cost can't be fully measured. In a world with significant devotion to the measurable, some executives may think that what is not measurable can't be that important. They may think it doesn't really matter. Maybe it doesn't matter for what's already in the past—but it certainly does matter for the future.

This tool, this strategy, is nothing new. In fact, it's as old as the human race. Anyone in a leadership position would intellectually be cognizant of it. The problem is, few have ever taken the time to study it, or more precisely, to actually understand it.

On the surface, this concept is deceptively simple, and that's a big part of the problem in having leaders embrace it. We think we know all about it. Because we think we know all about it, we would rather work around it. Avoid it. Work on something that seems much more sophisticated. Complexity makes us look smarter. And looking smarter is easier than being courageous. Executives in leadership positions can certainly fool most of the people most of the time. But this deception is ultimately wasteful. It wastes resources. More tragically, it wastes human potential and fulfillment. You can ignore it. But it will never ignore you.

The greatest tragedy is that we miss out on what is truly possible—personally as a leader, and collectively as an organization.

The strategy I've been talking about is a strategy based on core values, both in an organization and in an individual. In any organization, they are two sides of the same coin. Ultimately, it's this currency that matters most.

As we move forward, I hope the points I make will stir the conscience and consciousness of every leader at every level. Most importantly, I hope it will stir you on a personal level. I hope you will find our experience together to be challenging. It may even be a bit painful, but there will be huge rewards as a result. I can guarantee these rewards if you fully engage. I have no doubt you can take it. I hope you will also find this book to be relentlessly refreshing and a source of restoration—something many leaders probably need. Most importantly, I hope it will harness your desire to truly lead from your core; and I trust that once that powerful connection is made, you will never let go of it.

*　*　*

Before we begin, I want to get you started with a few reflections. These reflections are in no specific order, yet they are systemic just the same. They are simply here to prime the pump. Just to get you thinking from a lot of different angles—angles all pointed in one direction: toward your core!

[The New Veneer]

Over the past several years, there has been increasing chatter about core values. On the surface, this would appear to be a good thing. It may, in fact, prove to be one of the greatest obstacles we face in motivating leaders to address core values. You see, chatter stays exactly there—on the surface. Chatter can create a perception of focus and progress. Often it carries the deception of completion. One of the great challenges to solving a problem can be the perception that it has already been solved. My biggest fear is that core values have become the latest widespread veneer. Veneers are specifically designed to make something look like what it's not. The surface conceals what something is really made of—to make it look more valuable than it really is. Veneers work well on furniture, but not in organizations. If we discuss core values in only a shallow way, we allow the veneer approach to take hold. This is one of the reasons so many executives in leadership positions don't embrace core values. When core values are used as a veneer, they can clearly cause more harm than good. A lot more harm.

[From Band-Aids to Real Solutions]

Organizations have invested millions of dollars applying hasty solutions to the organizational development of alignment, employee engagement, productivity improvements, customer service, and retaining high performers. We have invested in sophisticated academic processes and methodologies to assess organizational vulnerabilities—only to address the issue with the application of a Band-Aid. We make the quick fix and then we move on to the next flavor of the month. We have invested in all but the one most promising solution: strengthening the condition of our core.

[Words Matter, But . . .]

There is no question that words matter. Words set the context for values. They allow us to communicate what we have come to agree upon and understand. It is not unusual for an executive leadership team to do an "off-site" meeting where they collectively articulate language that expresses the "stated core values" of an organization. Most often, however, the words they formulate remain just that. Simply words. But the true worth of core values is realized through our actions. A leader's greatest challenge is to strategically begin to live those words in action and then to lead others to do the same. Not for a moment. Not for a season. But day in and day out forever!

[Core vs. Attachments]

It has always amazed me how large trees can weather the most intense storms. Their root system provides enduring strength, and it helps them stand strong in the best and worst of circumstances.

Our core is like the root system of a tree. Among people, leaders are no different. It is our core that gives us the strength to lead. It enables us to endure the onslaught of daily storms and sustained periods of challenge. A strong core also enables us to manage our ego in the midst of sustained success.

A strong core holds us tight. If we are without a defined core, we likely hold tight to weak substitutes called attachments. These attachments come in many forms. Sometimes they are rules, policies, or procedures. Other times they are titles, positions, or power itself. For some, attachments are cliquish relationships. Attachments are the fertile ground where sacred cows are born.

When we cling to attachments, we tend to hold on to everything. Yet, embracing your core values allows you to give confidently. There is a great difference between the impact of attachments and the impact of living one's core values; the results couldn't be further apart.

[Why Bother?]

So why should we bother with building organizational value based on core values, especially when it won't be easy? It's a good question, one I have asked myself many times. It seems too hard. It sounds too vague. It feels too personal. It looks so un-businesslike! There has to be an easier path to lead others to success.

I could keep going with great excuses and credible roadblocks. I'm sure you could pile on your own reservations. I wouldn't blame you. In fact, I would encourage you. I have a list of my own! The fact is that it is much easier to figure out why building value with core values won't work than it is to actually build them.

As you continue to read, I hope you become so unsettled and then passionate that you can't resist embracing your role in leadership to show others precisely why to bother with it all. Only a leader who is actually leading can engage a collective confidence to create the traction and then the momentum needed to build value with core values.

[Why Now?]

But why now? Why is it so important that we act now? Because our world is changing significantly. That sounds like a cliché, but it is so true. It's true in organizations around the world, and it's true within various aspects of any organization. The single most significant change is speed. The speed at which we move. The speed at which decisions have to be made. The speed at which things change. And our world is in slow motion compared to the new world where we are headed!

The only way to respond to this exponential increase in speed is to know decisively who you are and what you do—personally and organizationally.

Beyond speed, another change we face is the progressively decentralized yet highly connected nature of organizations and the world. There are certainly some functioning hierarchical structures remaining in organizations, but the reality is that often these hierarchies are becoming more form than substance. Technology has significantly changed access to information and lines of communication inside and outside any organization.

We live in incredibly interesting times in business, in government, in churches, in communities, and in our homes. We haven't chosen these times; these times have chosen us. And even though these times are not our choice, they demand something from us nevertheless. I hope we'll deliver a response rather than a reaction. You might say that *Return On Integrity* is written precisely for such a time as this!

[The Value of Core Values]

The value of core values will show up in big and small ways. But here are three strategic areas where I'm certain any leader would be thrilled to see improvement:

- Achieving a natural alignment of every employee on every front

- Improving retention of your best people, whose authentic engagement is fueled by the intersection of individual and organizational values, with their engagement leading to personal fulfillment and organizational success

- Delivering customer/client service or patient experience by means of genuine and natural expression, rather than by a mechanical process

Collectively, these strategic enhancements add up to better performance.

[A Leader's Most Important Strategy]

Core values provide the content and framework for the most untapped and impactful organizational strategy available to any leader. It's not a complex strategy of intricate and complicated models. It's ruthlessly simple in nature, yet amazingly hard to sustain—unless you develop a depth of courage, patience, and persistence that can come only from an intentional connection to your own core.

Therefore, be clear: Connecting to your core values is strategic at the deepest level.

It is not a strategy to be forced upon others, but rather one that grows from within each individual. It is not an edict demanded from employees;

> **Therefore, be clear: Connecting to your core values is strategic at the deepest level.**

it is a calling forth, a call to greatness. It is a strategy that plants seeds. It doesn't demand alignment; this strategy grows it. It doesn't force employee engagement; this strategy nurtures it. It doesn't orchestrate a mechanical nature of "servicing" clients, customers, or patients; it ignites an individual desire to genuinely serve others.

It is a strategy that will make profound demands on you but will pay you back abundantly. It will create an ROI like you have never imagined possible.

But for most leaders, this strategy will require a shift in how deeply they understand, embrace, and engage the strategic potential of personal and organizational core values. It will require courage to sustain. Patience will be necessary. Persistence is a must. It will require all of who you are. The bottom line is that to succeed in this strategy, you have to be completely invested—and you have to stay invested!

[And So We Begin]

We have a lot of ground to cover—from your mind, to your heart, to your soul . . . and ultimately to your actions. I've divided our journey into three memorable experiences: *Dilemma*, *Definition*, and *Destiny*.

Dilemma

We'll begin right where we are—immersed in the reality of our current dilemma. I define our dilemma with a painfully honest analysis of why building value with core values can be so evasive. It does little good to have a strategic plan unless we fully understand the obstacles that stand in our way. Some of those obstacles are obvious roadblocks, and others are subtle or are like hidden land mines. It's important for us to open our eyes wide to that truth and to be fully aware of the individual and collective hurdles they present. Identifying these roadblocks and land mines isn't designed to stifle your enthusiasm, but rather to spark your creativity. As a reader and as a leader, choosing to stay in the middle of the dilemma before moving toward solutions will test your patience. You could certainly choose to skip forward to the definitive and prescriptive sections that follow. But this would present a significant level of risk, because understanding the dilemma is the first and most important part of the solution.

This dilemma can collectively loom large. I hope and trust that a leader would confidently acknowledge it and say, *Let's get started anyway*. It's important for us to be fully immersed in our reality before we proceed. It is where the momentum of courage, patience, and persistence is sparked.

Definition

Core values seem like a simple concept. But nothing could be further from the truth. They can become confusing quite quickly. We will discuss a framework and structure that will help you get your head around the mechanics of identifying your own personal core values and allow everyone in your organization to do the same. We will also discuss the flexibility that will be required every step of the way. We will investigate the current state of your organization's core values and show you how to institute a process of invigoration that identifies or re-identifies them and brings them to life. We will explore how you, as the leader, will lead that effort in a credible way. Your leadership in all of this begins precisely at the intersection of your own personal core values and the values of your organization. Regardless of the current condition of your own core, you can always create a new starting line. That starting line isn't only a good idea. You'll discover why it is the first and most critical step to success.

Destiny

So how do I get there? This final section is about destination. It's about where you are headed. It isn't about an end point. It's about your quintessential destiny, about who you will become, individually and organizationally, along the way. While it's important to brainstorm about what might be possible and to dream of those possibilities becoming reality, it's also important to have a road map to get there. Destiny is dependent on both. I like to think of this section as the *Destiny Road Map*. I'll provide the road map if you will provide the dream!

[Leadership Is the Linchpin]

There is no question that as a leader, you are the linchpin of this process. Building value with core values can certainly come from a grassroots effort. It's just not the ideal approach, and the results of this approach are rarely sustainable. It also undermines the credibility of leaders who have to be led to their own core by their followers!

Leaders, who lead, personally own this process. And when they do, amazing things begin to happen. This is your responsibility. No one else should do it for you. And the truth is, no one can. My question to you is, "Will you personally own it?" Where we are headed takes the committed vision of a leader. This book is not for followers in leadership positions. It is for leaders who genuinely want to lead!

I'll restate what I've said before: It won't be easy. In fact, there will be days when it will all seem impossible—which are precisely the days when you will realize that the only impossibility is not to push onward.

Generally when we think of ROI, most of us think of return on investment. But a time such as this demands a new definition of ROI that every investor, every board member, every leader, every employee, every customer, and every vendor should explore: *a Return On Integrity.*

Once you consciously experience your Return On Integrity, you will never see ROI in the same way again. And, by the way, the return on your investment will be amazing!

In the meantime, our dilemma looms. For real leaders, of course, the dilemma only makes the challenge all the more interesting.

Section 1:

Dilemma

Sometimes we're blind to the truth. Yet, our blindness doesn't change the truth. Our blindness simply has the potential to make us less than who we are. It puts us at a disadvantage. It diminishes our leadership.

I know what it's like to experience blindness. Two separate experiences with detached retinas in both eyes left me temporarily blind. The difference during those periods of blindness was that I was fully aware of my condition. I couldn't ignore it. In fact, in some ways, it brought its own blessings. I have often said to people, "When you are forced to keep both eyes closed for several days in a row, it's amazing what you will see!" I wouldn't wish that experience on anyone, but I'm convinced every leader's eyes would be opened if they found themselves in a state of temporary physical blindness.

But what we're talking about here is different. We are often unaware of our blindness to the truth. Sometimes we are blind to the truth because we simply don't stop long enough to see it. Sometimes we are blinded because we intentionally refuse to face it. Some people refuse to see the truth because of fear, some because of intellectual arrogance, others because it may demand a change, and still others because it's just more convenient that way. The specifics provided in this section aren't designed to overwhelm you in order to prove a point. In fact, certain specifics may not initially ring 100 percent factually accurate for you. I have included each of these ideas for consideration because I believe they have a very direct implication on our ability to discover our values, to understand them, own them, and consistently live them. These ideas are here to challenge you to open your eyes and look at the truth and where you may have been blinded to it or avoided it. It will take a real sense of vulnerability to look at some, if not all, of them. These specifics are not meant to be a comprehensive list but are meant to inspire you to brainstorm and create your own list. They are offered simply as possible dilemmas that might be standing in your way when it comes to building value with core values for yourself and your organization. Great leaders are hardwired with the insight and the courage to see the truth and the ability to lead others through the changes that truth demands.

Like someone turning on the light after being in a dark room, you may first squint reflexively. Slowly but surely, you will be able to open your eyes all the way. Once your eyes are open, your mind and eventually your soul will follow. From there, an amazing plan can emerge. The truth doesn't change, but it will change us.

1

Facing Realities

*The most dangerous undermining of any great movement
is to be blinded to the real obstacles as you begin.*

The first reality of pursuing a high Return On Integrity is that achieving it is not going to be easy. If it were easy, you would see it happening as the norm rather than the exception. The second reality is composed of endless small and subtle forces you will discover that are unique to your own situation and that lurk as roadblocks, obstacles, pushback, or undermining. The third reality is the mass of common, larger forces that create a systemic impact on everyone, either directly or indirectly. I call them boulders. If we take on the third reality first, it will shine a light on all the other realities we will eventually face along the way.

Boulders

Sometimes the obstacles that stand in the way of strategically building value with core values are very large ones. Sometimes very subtle ones. Often in and of themselves they are not bad things. In some cases, they are very good things. In most cases, they are just neutral. Nonetheless, they are boulders that can create quite a dilemma. It's only our blindness to their impact that creates a negative consequence.

[Assumptions]

The most subtle and dangerous boulder of all is assumptions! One of the greatest dilemmas we face when it comes to core values is, interestingly enough, the concept of core values itself. Intellectually, it is not a hard concept to grasp. It is not some sophisticated consultant methodology. But in today's workplace filled with volumes of management techniques, the concept of building value with core values can seem almost overly simplistic. When I address an audience on the sole topic of core values, my biggest concern is that they will shut down within the first two to three minutes. Why? Because many are likely thinking *Yeah, yeah, yeah, I know all about this core values stuff. I've heard about it so many times before.* And you know what? They're right! My question is, *Do we really* understand *the concept?*

The only approach to this dilemma is to take a second look every time we think we have already heard everything that can be said about it. In fact, the whole concept of building value with core values is unique precisely because you have to look at it again and again and again.

When it comes to core values, it is dangerous to assume almost anything, and we tend to leave a lot to assumption in this arena. We will discover just how much we do leave to assumption later on. But suffice it to say that for many, the most dangerous boulder we will face is the deceptively simple appearance of the concept of core values. The concept of core values is not designed to be an agenda item at your annual leaders retreat. It is the foundational design of your leadership. It doesn't require a few hours of your time. It demands your full attention.

> **The concept of core values is the foundational design of your leadership. It doesn't require a few hours of your time. It demands your full attention.**

[Technology]

Great innovation can cause its own dilemmas. Technology is one of those innovations. The exponential acceleration in the development of technology has been stunning, to say the least. It is hard to believe that most of the technology that drives the infrastructure of any size organization today didn't exist twenty-five years ago, and much of it didn't exist even ten years ago. This includes personal computers, mobile devices, the Internet, websites, email—and now, exploding social media. What did exist was very primitive and highly limited.

The dilemma of technology is amazingly subtle. Technology always comes packaged as an enhancement, a leap forward in efficiency and productivity. And very often it is just that. Social media can create the opportunity for connections. It can open the door to new relationships, both near and incredibly far away.

But, by definition, what social media does is create a context for developing shallow connections. In many cases, the environment it promotes is one of purely transactional relationships. It can eventually train us to operate solely on a surface level, not only with others but with ourselves as well. A plethora of shallow connections, an endless deluge of quick sound bites, and an ever-accelerating pace can push us stealthily to live on the surface of relationships, thoughts, and feelings. It can also coerce us to live in a place increasingly distant from our core.

Technology can dehumanize almost any environment. While it can make processes more productive, it can also make them less human. This is true for transactions as well as for entire work environments. Technology does bring speed and expanded capacity. But over time it can also lead to increasing human isolation. Technology and machines do not have core values; only humans do. Humans bring heart and soul to the workplace. That is, until technology imperceptibly begins to alter the human condition.

There is no stopping technology, which is precisely why personal core values and the core values of communities of people who make up organizations will only become all the more important.

[Measurements and Rewards]

Many new developments in the world have a major impact on core values and challenge our abilities to authentically know and live those values. One of these new developments is the pervasive ability to measure—far, deep, and wide—very quickly. And often. Very often. The speed and reach of present-day technologies take our ability to measure to a whole different level.

From a management perspective, it has been said that you get what you measure. The majority of measurements are designed to deliver the "what" an organization wants or needs, and this is most often tied to production and productivity. This "what" might be sales goals, chargeable hours, prospect contacts, product output metrics, measurements of call time, numbers of transactions in a call center—or the bottom line itself. Most types of measurement operate this way, and taking such measurements would appear to be a good thing. They are designed to drive intended outcomes and inspire behavior—whether by motivation or by fear. They certainly engage their own version of accountability. But they can also drive unintended outcomes and consequences. Often these consequences are the result of measurements that induce behaviors in direct or indirect violation of specific stated or intended organizational core values.

Core values have to drive measurements. If they do not, measurements retain the ability to completely drive out the values of an organization. We generally assume that the behavior induced by measurements will be appropriate, but in fact, the pressures of achieving a continuously measured benchmark can often undermine appropriate behaviors. This can sometimes happen overnight, but it usually takes place over time.

While the focus of measurement is generally objective, the design often ignores the subjective. One of the great strengths of measurements that are well designed is their ability to highlight key information. Yet, the strong emphasis on measurements can isolate the "what" that is being achieved from the all-important "how" it is being achieved.

As the management philosophy of measurement evolved, it eventually zeroed in on the concept of dashboard measurement. Like measurements themselves, the dashboard can be powerful—or powerfully destructive.

The problem isn't the measurement itself. The problem is the disconnect between values and measurement that arises when understanding, commitment, and engagement are not aligned with specific core values first. Values must steer the measurement process from the very beginning. Otherwise, intentional measurements will eventually create a strong set of unintentional organizational core values.

I do believe measurements are vitally important. You are more likely to achieve something if you establish a measure for it. The problem arises when you get unintended consequences that you don't plan for. In the absence of a deep connection to core values, the "how" in which you achieve the measurement becomes fair game, and the consequences, intended or not, eventually become destructive.

Unfortunately, all too often executives fail to reconcile the systemic play between values and measurements in their measurement-driven organizations.

Measurements have not only become numerous and precise; they have also become immediate. This immediacy can be a huge benefit in terms of fine-tuning or making course-changing adjustments that can instantly prevent incremental losses or can open the door for reaping desired results.

But the immediacy of measurements can also cultivate a very short-term mind-set, which can eventually nurture a very short-term culture. A short-term focus can produce disruptive, unproductive, and eventually disastrous results when its goal is to simply deliver a measurement or metric. It won't usually appear that way in the moment. It most often only becomes apparent when it's too late.

A short-term focus can be very healthy when it is consciously anchored in a deeply rooted set of core values and set in the context of a long-term strategy. It is even healthier when that connection is fully understood and embraced. Organizations can measure what seems like unlimited aspects of operations. But just because we can, doesn't mean we should! Every measure, large or small, has the potential to impact an individual's behavior, and therefore, eventually an organization's culture. This can be good if the measurements are founded and grounded within core values—or tragic if they are not.

With that said, the biggest dilemma of measurement today may have nothing to do with what, or even how, you measure. It has more to do with the fact that the most important things may not be quantifiably measurable by a computer at all. It's important to remember this when faced with management philosophies that espouse the philosophy that *if it's not measurable, it's not all that important.*

Certain supremely important concepts have to be unceasingly modeled and nurtured. And as a leader models them, they don't need a computer to measure them. Leaders will know it when they see it, and eventually, everyone else will too! A perfect example of this "it" is core values. I'm by no means advocating that you eliminate measurements! Keep in mind, however, that measurements are a lot less valuable and can eventually be destructive unless they are intentionally connected to a deep-rooted set of organizational values. They should be designed to embrace the values and not to undermine them.

The same is true for what you reward. Even more so! You get what you measure and reward; and when all your measurements and rewards are intentionally linked to your organization's core values, they become meaningful—and valuable.

People respond to measurements. They certainly respond to rewards. They respond with their decisions, their actions, and how they show up in relationships. When it comes to measurements and rewards, both need to stand the test of stated core values.

Not only do measurements and rewards need to stand the test of core values on the surface, they need to survive the analysis of unintended consequences. Unintended consequences can result in silos, internal competition that creates external problems, and shortcut gains at the expense of long-term failure.

Unintended consequences would be easy to manage if their cause was quickly apparent on the surface. If only these consequences could show their damaging potential from the start. But they don't. On the surface, they appear to be good and noble. Frequently, they have been allowed to persist with the best of intentions. But great intentions do not protect us from unintended consequences. If anything, they can blind us to how these choices and decisions regarding measurements and rewards are actually initiating a drift away from stated core values.

Let's say you create an impactful, well-founded set of measurements. But let's also say they are set into action in an organization that does not understand its core values or with employees who don't understand their own personal core values. Measurements are typically designed to drive results. Without the foundation of values, the pressure to achieve results can create leaks. I'm not talking about bad people doing bad things. I'm talking about good people drifting under pressure.

> **I'm not talking about bad people doing bad things. I'm talking about good people drifting under the pressure.**

It can also work in the other direction. Filtered choices, decisions, measurements, and rewards can celebrate the core values that mold the culture of any organization.

If it sounds like I'm bashing the measurement movement, I have clearly missed my mark. In fact, I believe core values are the epitome of true accountability. Measurements and rewards are dynamic tools that can help with our personal and collective accountability. But before undertaking any type of measurement, we must begin with a clear understanding of our personal values and the core values of our organization. These values should become our first and primary measurement, as they will ultimately determine how we achieve every other measurement.

We need to understand that measurements do make an impact. Therefore, they deserve their own test. It would serve us well to hold our measurements up to their own measurement!

[The Media]

Some of the greatest advancements in technology have advanced the capabilities of the media. Some of those media advancements have served us well. Others, not so much.

Reality TV may be a good place to start. It's a phenomenon that started small and seemed innocent enough. But it quickly evolved with increasing popularity to be a supplier of examples of selfish behavior to an ever-growing audience of addicted viewers. But it's just TV, right? Think again. It's not a sitcom. Granted, it's likely a mixture of staged drama and the reality it was originally dubbed. It often not only breeds the worst in our human condition; it rewards it. And even if you don't watch reality TV, you can bet many of those you lead—and measure—do.

More seriously, the television media's presentation of news has itself become the ultimate reality show. It may be more of a 24/7 microscope that has moved from the realm of journalism to sensationalism, and has taken the public with it. When you combine the decreasing length of the average viewer's attention span with 24-hour cable news, you concoct a formula of viewing that can be lethal to the truth. This format has basically made all of life a show. Ultimately, the real reality show!

This format creates a reactive rhythm. Brief and quick-moving segments often present information out of context or short of the full story. When viewers are subjected to the pressure of speed along with the spin that has been created to spark interest, our perspective is changed. The way we watch TV can diminish the value and undermine the integrity of the story all at once. I have always said that presenting a part of the truth is always a lie.

So what does this have to do with core values and organizations? I would propose *a lot*. On the surface, you would think it would create public accountability. In some cases, it might. Isn't that the noble purpose of journalism to begin with? In theory, yes . . . in reality, no. Especially when you have media organizations that have either questionable motives themselves or have leaders who haven't yet connected to their own core.

> **Leaders who become talented at spinning the story internally in their own organizations eventually get even more talented at spinning the story internally within themselves!**

This situation, in turn, puts all organizations in a defensive posture when they present their stories to the media, and eventually to everyone else. The media becomes masterful at spinning an organization's story to feed the public's addiction to sensationalism and, subsequently, that spin encourages others to spin the story some more. This creates an ever-growing web of deceit. When organizations get good at spinning their stories for the outside world, they become the ultimate masters at creating the same kind of messaging within their own organizations. Leaders who become talented at spinning the story internally in their own organizations eventually get even more talented at spinning the story internally within themselves!

This is a perfect example of how an external force can have an internal impact, and it illustrates why the habits of the media matter. I would like to think this impact is isolated only to organizations large enough to make the news. But habits become systemic and become part of the culture. Even if that weren't the case, speed and spin don't end with the networks. Round-the-clock cable news was just the beginning.

Next came a very different kind of media—social media. Social media makes 24/7 cable news look like slow motion. Social media contains its own version of well-spun representations of reality, posted for all to see. At the same time, it actually has a lot of potential when it comes to accountability to core values. In a rapid-fire display of sometimes unfiltered and unspun information, some of these postings provide an accountability trail of unintended public documentation of priorities, decisions, and behaviors. In social media, where all voices have equal airtime, the question becomes discerning between which voice is credible, and which is not.

This confusion often leads to a very reactive public conversation and sets up a platform for competing monologues rather than respectful dialogues. The public then faces the dilemma of how to separate out the difference between opinion, insight, and wisdom. Even if we could ignore the influence of the mainstream and the not-so-mainstream media along with the programming of reality TV, it's unwise to ignore the impact of social media. While those you lead are always watching, they are now, with social media, also posting what they see. And doing this changes behavior. It transforms the speed of communication and the flow of information. You would think, in some way, it would counteract the carefully spun communication of organizations, but often it creates more of it. The spin isn't coming only from the top; it is coming from every direction, with virtually none of it grounded in anything other than personal perspective and personal motives. In turn, it changes the mind-set in almost every organization.

Social media seems so innocent, doesn't it? But it's not. And you can't change it!

But you *can* lead an effort to intentionally embed values into the core of your organization.

In many organizations, values aren't the domain of leaders at all.

They are the product of internal media. If you are asking your marketing department to develop your core values, it's a huge problem!

Core values are not meant to be a brand. They may, along with everything else, influence the brand. But they are not your brand!

Your marketing professionals (whether they are an internal resource or an external provider) should not be permitted anywhere near the initial development of your core values. It is the responsibility of top leadership alone to do the hard work of grappling together until the truth of who they are begins to trickle from their heart

If you are asking your marketing department to develop your core values, it's a huge problem!

and soul. From there, a leader has the potential to open the floodgates of possibility.

Once the individual members of top leadership have found the essence of their own core and eventually the core of the organization, then and only then should marketing professionals assist in bringing emotion and impact to the language that will be used to express the genuine intent of their values. This should always take place under the watchful and discerning eyes of the leaders themselves. The responsibility and ownership of those core values should never fall into the hands of anyone else. Never, ever.

[Survival]

Economic success (or any version of success, for that matter) can create its own dilemma for staying anchored to your core. We have seen plenty of people at the height of success take a hard tumble. Staying grounded at your core is a critical paradox to confront while you are flying high!

Short-term economic pressure in an organization creates a very different kind of dilemma. This is especially true when the pressure is acute and when the conditions are about economic survival. Sometimes these

conditions are clearly apparent, and sometimes they are relatively perceived. Regardless, short-term economic issues can bring significant
stress, pressures, or demands that are very real. These challenges place
enormous strain on everyone—especially those without an intentionally
defined set of core values.

Economic survival also brings into focus the paradox of core values.
Over a number of years, we have done a great disservice to the concept of
core values. We have made them the soft, touchy-feely wall coverings for
hallways and conference rooms. We have created an image of core values
as those nice things to look to when it's convenient. They are subject
matter for the conversations at management retreats. We have thought of
them as the sweet side of a tough business world.

The truth is, core values are anything but the contents of a candy dish.
They form the backbone of every leader who chooses to have one. Core
values aren't about making nice, easy decisions. Nor are they your excuse
to avoid tough decisions. They are your asset in every decision you make,
and they bring their greatest value when the decisions are the toughest.

Nice decisions are for short-term convenience and have no grounding
in core values. Hard decisions, made through the context of core values,
will get you to the right decision in a credible way. Tough economic conditions do create a sole focus on survival, especially in the absence of a
defined core. That focus on survival creates a scarcity mind-set and leads
ultimately to isolation and silo-minded thinking. It ignites shortsighted
decisions that have very real long-term impacts.

On the other hand, an environment where defined core values are
strong turns the worst economic challenges into opportunities for development and creativity. An even stronger organization emerges on the
other side of the storm.

Core values give purpose and meaning to everyone in the organization. They consistently remind the leadership, management, and employees alike that all the blood, sweat, and tears spent in the fight to survive

were worth it. They were worth it because in the end everyone involved comes to realize the organization that was saved was truly worth saving.

[Addictive Greed and Entitlement]

Addiction comes in all shapes and sizes. It knows all economic strata and every demographic. It can hook us at our weakest link or at the place of our greatest desire. Addiction can be particularly lethal because it overtakes its victim in slow, sly, and subtle ways. Addiction comes from continual *addition*. Ironically, *addition* is the same word as *addiction*, without the letter *c*. You might say that addiction is caused by addition that you don't *c*—or see! Unfortunately, the addicted are usually the last to see, or to realize, or to ultimately admit to their addiction.

An addiction can manifest in many ways. Sometimes it shows up as a healthy but growing confidence that lethally morphs into overconfidence, and eventually into arrogance. Other times, an addict moves from having a sense of genuine gratitude for the success achieved, to the sense that the success was well deserved, and finally to the delusion that success was owed to him. Ungrounded and unchecked, this delusion can lead to a place of greed and entitlement.

Leaders at the top—CEOs, presidents, entrepreneurs—often share a common dilemma. As with most addicts, they are often the last to see and admit their addictions. They are also the least likely to be told about them by other people. We see this same phenomenon with movie stars, recording artists, professional athletes, top government officials, and religious leaders. No one in the inner circle wants to be kicked out for telling the truth, and so the addiction begins to spread. If a leader can't see the addiction and no one confronts her about it, nothing arrests its spread.

Addictions of this kind rarely stem from greed or entitlement. They start with an honest commitment to hard work and an endless passion for that work. Somewhere along the way, something changes imperceptibly. Frequently, for many in key positions, the addiction is grounded in the belief that success has been hard-fought and rightfully earned—and often it has been. The biggest dilemma in the addiction is that it's born from conditions rather than intention.

The development of addiction creates a gap between who we really are and what we have become. This gap leads to entitlement. Like addiction, entitlement knows no economic or demographic boundary. In the economic boom of the 1990s, *Fast Company* magazine tucked a powerful question into the lower corner of the cover of a monthly issue. It simply asked, *When is enough enough?* It is an important question that few people (including many executives) can answer. It sounds limiting. But paradoxically, answering it is quite empowering. It's a matter of richness rather than riches.

When is enough enough?

If you have an executive who cannot answer this question, who has no clearly defined personal core, who has had a virtually uninterrupted run of success—you can bet greed and entitlement are often just around the corner. There is nothing wrong with success. But what you do with your success is certainly influenced by the answer to that simple question: *When is enough enough?* No one, generally, decides to embrace greed or a sense of entitlement. We are generally blind to it. And it is blinding to us. It is especially blinding when it comes to our core.

It is greed and entitlement that drive us to a place where we end up needing what we want rather than wanting what we need. So imagine what happens when followers . . . follow the leader!

Greed and entitlement are very different from reaping the rewards of our lifetime of effort and results. Rewards can motivate us. Greed and entitlement change our motives.

Over time, they literally redefine our core, whether we are aware of it or not. When we are not connected to our core, it is only a matter of time until our core becomes connected to something else.

This is especially true for leaders, because most leaders are on the path to success. When leaders haven't answered the powerful question of when enough is enough, they become vulnerable. At some point, they are no longer on the path of success. They are on the highway to greed and entitlement. It would be easy and appropriate to shine the spotlight on the downfalls of highly touted corporations such as Enron. I'm sure you could take your choice of celebrity, athlete, or athletic program. The risk of using such celebrated cases, however, is that it nurtures our belief that this addiction happens only in cases of runaway

> **When we are not connected to our core, it is only a matter of time until our core becomes connected to something else.**

success. However, this is a very dangerous perspective, as it feeds the notion that this addiction is about *other* leaders in *bigger* arenas. I would propose it is about every leader. The size of the arena is irrelevant when it comes to the potential for addiction of a leader and the potential for the harm it can cause to all they lead. Addiction can happen in a backyard nonprofit. I am sure you could think of a few of those stories too. Every one of us is susceptible to a runaway sense of how much is enough. If there is anything that can guarantee the derailment of organizational alignment, employee engagement, and customer service among employees, it is the conscious or subconscious belief that a leader is filled with greed and has a sense of entitlement. It makes no difference whether the leader is blinded to it or not. The employees will see it with 20/20 vision. This is personally devastating for any leader, and it is also the recipe for organizational disaster.

Asking the question *When is enough enough?* isn't about creating limitations. It is about establishing a grounded perspective. Leaders can't simply decide they are not going to fall prey to greed and entitlement. They have to protect themselves with a deep sense of their own personal values that have been purposefully connected to the values of the organization they lead, and with a relentless commitment to live those values each and every day.

It can be a terrifying experience to face your core—to find out who you really are—when you have become someone different from the person you used to be. Most successful leaders haven't been "required to" intentionally identify their core, so they don't. And everyone pays the price for that. This is an unnecessary dilemma that every leader needs to seriously and honestly face. Especially since there will likely be no one standing in line to tell them so.

[Globalization]

The highly connected global community seems more like an opportunity than a dilemma. Yet, it's both. Advancements in transportation and technology have changed the global landscape. It is a small world after all. And it can create significant confusion as organizations go from competing with other organizations around town, to competing with other organizations around the world, to eventually becoming an organization spanning the globe. This isn't future shock. It is today's reality. We are bringing together people from different cultures in a way that brings the concept of diversity to an exponentially different level. There is often no common denominator or any common experience. As we bring macro cultures together from around the world, they have an impact on the micro cultures of an organization. These mosaic macro cultures shouldn't be left unchecked to unintentionally evolve a set of core values. Core values should be intentionally clarified to create a healthy organizational culture filled with a rich diversity. Some in global organizations would say it is very difficult to define core values in the context of such different cultures. I would agree it is a dilemma that makes core values all the more valuable. It also opens the door to an opportunity of defining a core that is much richer than ever before and certainly more necessary!

The process of defining core values moves an organization beyond the practice of making assumptions across borders. Establishing, understanding, and owning a defined core can be accomplished only as a result of discussions and clarifications across an often wide array of life experiences. The process promotes understanding instead of judgment.

In addition to the cultural diversity of globalization, there is a great paradox at work. In the midst of an organization with tentacles around the globe, thousands of daily decisions are being made at the tips of those tentacles. Decentralization is a reality. You might say it is both large and local. Many organizations have spent significant dollars on methodologies, processes, and procedures to curb the risk of this decentralized decision making. Methodologies will never create a core, but an unintentional core will certainly create some methodologies. Unfortunately, those ad hoc methodologies have the potential to deliver a very unintended and disconnected global organizational culture.

[The Blender]

The evolution of a globalized business community unleashes an opportunity for a rash of mergers and acquisitions just down the street. While we call them mergers and acquisitions, they more likely resemble blended families—just a lot more complex! This blend can be more challenging than reaching into different cultures around the globe. In those cases, differences are pretty blatant. Often, in the case of mergers and acquisitions, differences are far more subtle, often whitewashed over, and therefore more pernicious. Whether you call it a merger or an acquisition, a new entity is created. Either situation creates a natural opportunity to redefine the core of the newly formed organization. The redefinition should be one of the *first* items of discussion in the merger/acquisition process, rather than one of the last items on the checklist before the deal is sealed.

In these situations, two unfortunate results can happen. The merged group can feel forced into something it is not, or the acquiring group can pretend it is still the same as it was. Both outcomes create problems. Taking the opportunity to redefine the core for everyone unleashes a refreshed

The ever-increasing size of organizations, often through mergers and acquisitions, makes the need for core values all the more relevant and valuable.

potential for all. Beyond the blending of cultures, the increased size of the organization can create its own dilemma. There is simply not enough methodology in change management to overcome the challenges that can come with size when there is not a defined set of core values. The ever-increasing size of organizations, often through mergers and acquisitions, makes the need for core values all the more relevant and valuable.

[Generations]

Never before have so many generations been simultaneously in the active workforce. Some would estimate that today's workforce spans four or five generations. Others would add that not only does the quantity of generations create a challenge, but also the differences between them exponentially increase that challenge.

It seems an entire industry of consultants, speakers, and books has been focused on the differences between these generations. Many important insights have surfaced from the examination of these differences; yet, while it's important to note them, it's destructive to dwell upon them.

The dilemma here isn't the generations. The dilemma is our dwelling on their surface-level differences without digging deeper. Generations by definition are lumped into generalizations, and generalizations have a way of pulling us to the surface. When you combine the dwelling on differences with the absence of an intentional awareness of personal core values, you create an even greater divide between generations.

Staying on the surface of anything or anyone will always lead you to a set of differences, disconnects, and unhealthy divides—especially when that is what you're looking for.

I think we would be surprised to find that the deeper we dig into the core values of individuals within each generation, the more we might find how much they have in common. The differences we've always seen might give way to a significant number of similar core values across generations.

Starting with what is different between the generations takes you on a very different path than first digging for what they have in common.

[Religious Myth]

I would classify this next dilemma as a misconception or a myth. It also makes for a convenient excuse—or an out. Some people will push back on focusing on core values in the marketplace because they feel core values might be a bit religious in nature. I could see from a surface perspective how thinking about core values might make someone leap to that conclusion. Values are about deep convictions, but they are different from a theology.

I would challenge this perspective with practical proof. If core values are religious, then why do so many religious institutions have the same human struggles as any secular organization? The truth is the other way around. The leader of any religious organization would be just as well served as any marketplace leader to journey the same pathway to personal and organizational core values. All leaders may very well find it to be a deeply spiritual experience. It may very well help them deepen their faith and more deeply live the faith they have.

[Excuses]

We are likely to do anything to justify viewing core values as just a sidebar rather than the most untapped and impactful resource all leaders have at their disposal. It is convenient to see core values as just another thing rather than the main thing. The main thing of everything. It is always easier to write off something as insignificant, or assume it won't work. It's convenient, because in doing so, we can move on to the next thing on our list—something "worthy" of our leadership position. We don't have to do anything further about it. Writing it off won't demand anything from

> **It takes a great leader to intuitively understand and creatively lead an idea to its full potential. That is certainly the case with core values.**

you in the short run; yet, it may take everything from you in the long term.

It takes a great leader to intuitively understand and creatively lead an idea to its full potential. That is certainly the case with core values.

*   *   *

By the very nature of this *Dilemma* section of *Return On Integrity*, I believe it's incredibly helpful to be realistic about the boulders standing in the way. I want to encourage you to use this sample list of various dilemmas to further stimulate your thinking. Have at it. Dig deep in searching for pebbles and boulders alike. Be creative and innovative. More important, be deeply honest. Start with yourself, but don't keep it to yourself. Invite others in your leadership circle into the process. Have them push hard as well to reveal every dilemma they can think of. Leave no stone unturned. You might be amazed what you learn in that process alone. Falling into the trap of "excuses" might very well be one of them.

This exercise isn't designed to be discouraging, although at times it might feel that way. Quite the opposite. It is actually required to embolden you and encourage you to realistically own and fully embrace the leadership required for the important work ahead.

It positions you to proactively lead. Anything short of this positions you to reactively follow while sitting in a position of leadership. Some dilemmas are bigger than boulders. So let's keep going.

Bottom Line

It's hard to go any further without having an honest conversation about the bottom line. Let's just say it's the elephant in the room.

Some would suggest that when it comes to core values, the bottom line is the biggest dilemma of them all. Others would say it's the dilemma that creates all the other dilemmas. It might be, but not always for the reasons you think.

Some believe the financial bottom line is the only real core value of their organization in the marketplace. And in a number of cases, it would surely appear that way. Some executives honestly see things that way. It is what they believe and how they operate. Frankly, this book wasn't written for them. It is unlikely I will convince them otherwise; however, a personal or professional tragedy just might.

But executives aren't the only ones who believe that the bottom line is a core value. There can be a group of cynical employees who further the assertion that executives value only the bottom line. Often, it is these employees who engage in the tactic of wearing blinders to release themselves from the responsibility of living the stated core values of the organization. It takes them off the hook for a whole lot of personal accountability. It can be a very convenient perspective!

Frankly, this book wasn't written for them either. By declaring themselves victims, they already live in the midst of a personal and professional tragedy. Usually their only way out is to luck upon a leader with a valuable core who will lead them out of their self-imposed dilemma.

The financial bottom line is an area where many perceptions are formed and many motives are questioned. To fully embrace building values with core values, we have to come directly at this issue. In the absence of a pointed conversation and understanding concerning this issue, there is no question that the financial bottom line becomes the default core value—whether we intend it to be or not!

[Profit Is Not a Core Value]

Profit is a good thing. In fact, it's a really good thing! It is also a necessary thing if you want to keep your dream, mission, and vision fully alive.

Later we will talk about core values vs. needs vs. wants vs. behaviors, and how each of them is critically important. These are not four distinct black-and-white categories. But they do have distinct characteristics. And in some cases, it is important to make that distinction clear. That is especially true when it comes to the issue of bottom-line profit.

For some, this will be really hard to read. Perhaps you should take a deep breath first. It's certainly hard to write—not because I don't believe it, but because I believe so many executives in leadership positions will have a hard time reading it and honestly processing it at first. They won't be the only ones.

Let me repeat: *Profit is not a core value.*

Profit is not a core value.

I realize it may be presumptuous on my part to tell anyone else whether something is a core value or not. And in fact, profit may be the only thing I would take a stand on. When it comes to core values vs. needs vs. wants vs. behaviors, there are some very subjective personal calls that need to be made between the categories. But bottom-line profit is different.

When profit is a core value, all other core values become secondary. Not initially. But eventually. Profit will demand its own priority. And if it doesn't, you certainly will bestow top priority upon it. It won't happen overnight. It rarely does. It will subtly happen over time. It will become an obsession when times are tight, and an addiction when times are bright. And to make matters worse, when it comes to profit, giving the bottom line top stature subtly evolves for "noble" reasons.

Obsession with profit, or addiction to it, eventually becomes the enemy of core values. In fact, it often encourages and enables behavior that undermines core values. Ultimately, this obsession defines its own set of core values and a deadly partnership is formed.

Our attention to the bottom line is important. But too much of a good thing can become a terrible thing. If you want to create a seductive dilemma, put profit anywhere within your core.

In my many years at Arthur Andersen, we had seven shared values: Quality Service, Quality People, Meritocracy, One-Firm Approach, Integrity, Innovation, and Stewardship. We also had four Cornerstones: Clients, People, Risk, and Profit. While the seven core values were well ingrained into the culture, some would say that instead of four cornerstones, the firm really had three pebbles and a boulder. You can probably guess which of the four cornerstones was perceived as the boulder!

Bottom-line profit was measured by earnings per unit, or EPU. EPU was a critical number in the budgeting process—as it should have been! It was important. But how important can profit become before it has a negative, systemic impact on all other aspects of the organization? No measurement stands alone. The fact of the importance of profit was not the problem. The desire that it be higher and higher, year after year, was a problem.

Just so you don't read between the lines, I am not saying this EPU boulder eventually caused the demise of Arthur Andersen. The demise of Arthur Andersen is far more complicated than that, and had as much to do with those on the outside of the firm as it did with anyone on the inside.

I will say this: The focus on continually increasing the EPU expectations certainly put a strain on the partners, culture, and values of the firm. But in this regard, Arthur Andersen was certainly not unique. It's not only naive, but extremely dangerous to assume so.

Some would say that Arthur Andersen became a corrupt culture. I strongly disagree. I would put the quality of that firm's culture and its professionals up against any organization that has ever existed in a capitalistic society. The fact that the demise of Andersen happened in the midst of an exemplary culture ought to be a wake-up call to any and every leader.

The "profit boulder" is not only an issue with for-profit companies.

The same mind-set, ironically, can also permeate the culture of any not-for-profit organization.

Likewise, it can steal the soul of a religious organization. The reality is, it can steal the soul of any organization, beginning with anyone who leads it!

[Profit Is a Core Need]

While profit is not a core value, it *is* a core need. In fact, if you want to really challenge organizational and personal core values, just let the bottom line start profusely bleeding. Become irresponsible with keeping tabs on results—not only will you have neglected the bottom line, you likely will have neglected several of your core values.

You could compare profit to sleep. I don't know of anyone who lives so they can sleep. I realize we all have days where complete exhaustion may make getting to sleep the be-all and end-all, but that's the exception. I certainly don't think many leaders would care to hang out with people who would make sleep their highest priority. At the same time, we all know that we can't live without sleep. Sleep deprivation has very predictable, devastating consequences over time.

Several years ago, I was visiting a great friend in Seattle. After dinner we went to hear a guest lecturer at the University of Washington. He was literally a brain scientist. While he covered numerous aspects of the brain, the fact I remembered most was the incredible impact that sleep has on the brain. While sleep certainly restores your body, the greatest benefit of sleep is the restoration of your brain!

Sleep is critical to the functioning of the brain. It impacts memory, critical-thinking skills, and your ability to think creatively. Sleep allows the brain to process, sort, and store information for retrieval at a later point.

Yet, as important as sleep is to the functioning of the brain, we don't live to sleep. In fact, too much sleep would eventually diminish and destroy the very thing it is designed to support—the health of the very core of your body. Muscles would become weak, breathing would become shallow, and vital organs would begin to shut down. The same is true for profit. It is a bit of a paradox. Something so critical to funding and keeping the dream of an organization alive is the very thing that will destroy that organization if it becomes the be-all and end-all—if it becomes a core value.

[Core Values and the Bottom Line Aren't Enemies]

Somehow, we have created two camps, positioning the bottom line and core values as enemies of each other. Mutually exclusive. Or, at best, at extreme ends of the same continuum.

There are the hardliners who view core values as nothing more than eye candy for the lobby walls. They view core values as the soft ingredients used for sweet conversations on executive retreats. They often tout their own intellect, their sophistication, and their business savvy as the measure of their worth. They might consider themselves the providers for those poor souls who get hung up on the soft stuff. They tolerate a nod, every now and then, to such fluff and glitter if they must. But for them it is all about profit, and anything that gets in the way is a wasteful distraction. After all, business is business.

On the other end sit the cynical, righteous, judgmental victims who roll their eyes at the core values on the lobby wall. They *say* core values are important, yet they gossip about how the values in the lobby aren't real. They personally violate many of them every day with their fellow employees as they shirk the responsibilities for which they are compensated. They believe any focus on the bottom line or profit is, by definition, a violation of core values—if not of human rights.

Granted, these are extremes. Clinging to these extremes undermines the valuable connection between profit and core values. They are not enemies of each other. They serve each other; in fact, they have the potential to serve each other quite well. And it behooves all of us to creatively understand their connection and the support they can give each other.

It is interesting to note how often money is addressed in the Bible. In his Gospel, Matthew clearly calls out the essence of the issue at hand: "For where your treasure is, there your heart will be also" (Matthew 6:21). It wasn't a condemnation of money. It was a note to the wise as to the role money plays in our life.

The Bible also makes it clear that money is not the problem. Many people have misquoted the Bible when they say it demonizes money. It is convenient for them to do so, since misquoting puts the blame on money. You will often hear, "Money is the root of all evil." But that is not what the Bible says.

The Bible actually says, "The *love* of money is the root of all kinds of evil" (Timothy 6:10). Money doesn't love. We do. So what, then, is the real problem—people or money?

The Bible also addresses our responsibility for the resources we have been given. It is seen in the "Parable of the Talents" (Matthew 25:14–30), as told by Jesus. The translation as expressed in *The Message* highlights this responsibility:

> "It's also like a man going off on an extended trip. He called his servants together and delegated responsibilities. To one, he gave five thousand dollars; to another, two thousand; to a third, one thousand, depending on their abilities. Then he left. Right off, the first servant went to work and doubled his master's investment. The second did the same. But the man with the single thousand dug a hole and carefully buried his master's money.
>
> "After a long absence, the master of those three servants came back and settled up with them. The one given five

thousand dollars showed him how he had doubled his investment. His master commended him: 'Good work! You did your job well. From now on be my partner.'

"The servant with the two thousand showed how he also had doubled his master's investment. His master commended him: 'Good work! You did your job well. From now on be my partner.'

"The servant given one thousand said, 'Master, I know you have high standards and hate careless ways, that you demand the best and make no allowances for error. I was afraid I might disappoint you, so I found a good hiding place and secured your money. Here it is, safe and sound down to the last cent.'

"The master was furious. 'That's a terrible way to live! It's criminal to live cautiously like that! If you knew I was after the best, why did you do less than the least? The least you could have done would have been to invest the sum with the bankers, where at least I would have gotten a little interest.

"'Take the thousand and give it to the one who risked the most. And get rid of this "play-it-safe" who won't go out on a limb.'"

Core values are not the enemy of profit—or vice versa. In fact, strong core values, when lived strategically and consistently, will become profit's best friend in creating a meaningful bottom line. Core values will bring health to the bottom line. They will also equip

Core values are not the enemy of profit—or vice versa.

everyone to maintain a healthy perspective about the value of the bottom line. The bottom line here is . . . profit is not the problem.

The bottom line here is . . . profit is not the problem.

Profit, ultimately, is about stewardship. It is about taking on the responsibility of being a good steward of the resources available to you. It's about leaving any organization better than you found it. The bottom line can be an effective measure of that stewardship. It allows for reinvestment and creates a rightful return on investment for all who have invested.

The question isn't whether the bottom line is important. The issue at hand is at what cost it is achieved. Most often, when there is an obsession with profit, the cost is at the expense of some, and eventually all, core values.

Sleep enables the brain to keep functioning. Likewise, profit allows an organization to keep functioning. Understanding your core values and truly living them allows you to sleep much better. More on that later!

[Misplaced Motivation]

I sometimes see top executives touting a focus on the bottom line as an inspirational focal point to get people excited. When the bottom line is grounded in core values that are genuinely embraced, it can be inspirational. Generally, however, these top executives attempt motivational rallies to reflect their own excitement for a booming bottom line or their desperate call to action for a bottom line that's busting. Disconnected from a meaningful set of core values, however, neither angle really rallies the troops. If anything, it demotivates them. The only one motivated is the executive delivering the message.

There is a paradox at play here. By making profit the top priority, you undermine its sense of priority at all. The stakeholders—other than direct owners (entrepreneurs, partners, or shareholders)—are inspired only when they believe owners genuinely care more about something besides the bottom line. And when they are convinced owners care more about that something, they are more likely to be genuinely pleased when the results of the bottom line are plentiful, and inspired to do something about the bottom line when it's not ideal.

There are some executives who admit that the bottom line is their driving top priority. Other executives just pretend that something else is the top priority. But followers are never fooled. Not for long, anyway.

As a leader, you have to dig deeper. There is more to you than that, and to think otherwise is selling yourself short on your true potential, your ultimate responsibility, and your call to fulfillment. Let me be clear. I am not advocating that you forget about profit. That would be contrary to any sense of stewardship. In fact, I am advocating that when you become fully aware of your personal values and their intersection with your organization's core values, your bottom line will get better rather than worse. It's just a matter of knowing where to place your focus. It's a question of what leads and what lags.

> **It's a question of what leads and what lags.**

You have no idea how much I wanted to delete this section from the book. I know there is a chance it could be misconstrued. But I also know obsession with profit is the most common boulder preventing us from genuinely and strategically building value with core values. Some leaders know it, but I think we would all prefer to pretend it just isn't true.

Unfortunately, our preferences and our pretenses just don't change the truth! They only avoid it. I know this is a tough pill to swallow. Don't even try. As you continue to read, chew on it for a while. As you dive deeper into the value of core values, keep chewing—eventually, you will find this pill much easier to swallow!

And in the meantime, take a look at yourself and ask if your current situation is breeding an obsession with the bottom line.

Distance and Disconnection

There is a greater dilemma at play. This one will feel distant. It will feel more like a mirage than something tangible. It can feel overwhelming in nature . . . impossible to get your arms around. Since I launched my speaking career in 1996, I always wanted an element of my presentations and books to be practical and actionable. But the real mission of my work was simply to get you thinking. I have always trusted that once participants in my audiences and readers of my books started thinking in a deeper way, clarity would come to them on the practical and actionable steps they would need to take. Admittedly, you may find nothing immediately practical or actionable in this next section. But I hope it gets you thinking! This dilemma isn't about a few bad people. It would be much easier if it were. It's much worse than that. It's about millions of totally unaware, disconnected, good people.

This dilemma isn't about a few bad people. It would be much easier if it were. It's much worse than that. It's about millions of totally unaware, disconnected, good people.

I fully understand the wisdom in focusing on what you can control. Yet sometimes, as leaders, we also need to understand a greater context. This context is simply about distance. First, it's about the distance between short term and long term. Second, it's about the distance between individual investors and ultimate decision makers. And third, it's about the distance between expectations and consequences. All of these have come to exist within the context of something good. It is a fundamental need for public companies to rally the capital needed to invest and develop great opportunities. This system has created an empowering economic engine, which in turn has brought ideas to the light of day. Public companies have created jobs and career opportunities that would have been impossible to imagine in prior generations.

These opportunities have been built on the backs of many, and from the pocketbooks of willing risk-takers. They have evolved from the depths of passion, creativity, sacrifice, and an undying commitment to build and grow. Yet, the more companies evolve, and the larger they get, the more distance is created from top to bottom, side to side, and everywhere in between. And that can create dilemmas—of distance and disconnection.

[Between Short Term and Long Term]

The speed at which we move changes the distance between the short term and the long term. There was a time when not much would change in a company over an entire decade. I remember when an organization would talk about a change for a year—to warn everyone it was coming! In today's world ten things would significantly change in the same time frame, with no warning at all.

When only a little changes in ten years, the distance between short term and long term is not very far. The faster things change, the greater the distance between short-term decisions and long-term implications. It is the exponential increase in the volume of changes—within the same span of time—that creates a totally different relative gap between the short term and long term. Today's executives are often accused of sacrificing the long term to achieve a short-term result. This might seem justifiable with today's emphasis on measurement. Yet, it ultimately clouds the issue. The quality of a decision isn't based on alignment to the short term or long term. The quality is defined by the alignment to a set of intentional core values. Where core values are clear and universally embraced, the distance between the short term and long term becomes irrelevant. Where there are no stated values, or where stated values are window dressing or deliberately ignored, there will be bad decisions that are not good for the short term or the long term, regardless of the distance in between.

[Between Investors and Decision Makers]

I imagine the embryonic stages of capitalism were pretty simple. It might have gone something like this. You and I have a great idea, yet we don't have any resources. We do, however, have a great friend who has no ideas, yet, for whatever reason, has resources. So our friend makes an investment in us. At the time, it's likely our friend was just hoping to get his money back—or at least some of it!

Our friend invested because of the closeness of our relationship and because he believed in us. And because of the relationship, we wanted to honor the investment and confidence our friend had placed in us to enable our idea to see the light of day.

There wasn't a lot of distance between any of us. We saw one another all the time. The return for our "joint-venture capitalist" was getting to see the progress of our idea and knowing we all played a part in it. It was essentially about relationship and participation.

Today there is no relationship or participation. Things have evolved to be all about the return. Are things better or worse? Actually, a lot of things became better. More sophisticated. More efficient. Bigger ideas with increased scalability. But all of this increased the distance—the distance between the decision makers and the everyday investor.

Without the sense of relationship or participation, the only return left for the investor is the desired return on investment, and usually that means the more the better. I'm not here to judge if this is better or worse. I'm here to say the nature of investing and investors has evolved to something significantly different.

You might say that in creating scalability of ideas, this nature of investing has also scaled itself. And this scalability has created a significant distance between the decision makers and the everyday investor. This distance diminishes and eventually eliminates relationships and meaningful participation. It changes the motive, the expectations, and ultimately the demands of the investors. It makes the need for core values all the more important. You might say the value of core values becomes all the more valuable. When it was just you, me, our ideas, and our great friend "investing" their belief and a few dollars, we would pull up some chairs together on a front porch and discuss our challenges, roadblocks, and successes; and we knew what defined our core through our firsthand relationships with one another.

The stock market grew far beyond the neighborhood. I have no doubt a few close friendships were forever ruined when great ideas turned out to be not so great and all was lost. Initially, some amount of distance was probably a good thing.

As the stock market grew, greater levels of accountability drove the creation of more efficient and effective organizations. The context of this evolution was a relatively stable environment of limited organizational changes from year to year. Management and their employees settled in for lifetime careers. Their stability defined the predictability that characterized the organization. And investors simply assumed and expected that character. While distance in miles grew, their mind-sets remained close.

For the most part, that's all in the distant past. The distance between investors and decision makers is far greater now. Not only in miles, but in expectations and mind-set. And if that's not complicated enough, everything is far more fluid. Not only do executives and employees come and go on a regular basis—so do investors.

Distance can create a dilemma, especially when you combine it with an endless number of changing players. Without core values, this dilemma can lead to disaster. It begins by attacking parts of the whole. Left unattended, it's only a matter of time before it systematically affects the entire whole and eventually destroys it. With actual individual shareholders, regardless of distance, the situation is a little different. They are still a defined population who have decided to invest directly. You can find and communicate with them. As hard as it might be, you can get long arms around it.

This is a challenging enough proposition in a private corporation, in a partnership, or with a single entrepreneur. It becomes increasingly complicated in a large publicly held company. We will explore this issue in just a bit.

[Between Expectations and Consequences]

As the stock market evolved, distance and new options became greater. For most people, investing in the stock market was not only out of reach, but the risk involved made it irresponsible. The average individual didn't have the financial sophistication, the fiscal risk tolerance, or the time to be a responsible investor. The market, in relative terms, was reserved for just a few.

And then a great idea surfaced that would allow a much broader group to participate in the market. Many would be able to make responsible investments, because they would no longer need financial sophistication. The risk of investing would significantly diminish—or at least it would be spread around. All it took was a responsible commitment to save money. It was a revolutionary idea that seemed to be a win-win for all. It was called mutual funds. Great ideas can have unforeseen and unintended consequences, especially when they prove to be wildly successful. Even if you bring the fruit of the capital markets to the masses, transform an irresponsible investment into a responsible form of savings, and spread the risk, you can still create a dilemma.

Mutual funds take the concept of distance to a whole new level. In fact, there is really no definable distance, because there is no real connection between the initial investor and the ultimate recipient of the investment. It would be hard to know whom to invite to a conversation on the front porch. Mutual funds are composed of unrelated forces, all with different motives, bound together by money alone.

The mutual funds phenomenon created a momentum that pulled together massive pools of capital. Fund managers have enormous responsibility to shepherd those funds and generate the one thing most owners of these mutual funds care about: return, lots of return. These "investors" have an endless appetite for more and more.

And these "investors" are pretty much everyone who owns a 401(k).

In 2012, more than 52 million Americans had 401(k)s. And virtually none of them know where their funds are actually invested. Fund managers certainly understand the impact of metrics and measurements. They live and die by their "return" performance. It would seem the future retirement livelihood of millions of Americans is on their backs. That's a lot of weight to carry. The real truth is that the future quality of retirement life for millions of Americans is on the backs of hundreds of organizations trying to productively deliver returns to the concentrated pools of 401(k) capital. That pressure is very real, and consistently delivering that expectation can put a lot of pressure on core values.

Much good has come from millions being able to participate in what was once an investment arena accessible by only a few. The unintended consequences of mutual funds are the enormous concentrated pools of capital that are constantly shifting in an attempt to reach the "return performance" expected of these money managers.

If you factor in advancements in technology and the related impact brought through automated computer trading, we find ourselves in a completely different world from where the seeds of capitalism were planted. Is that a bad thing? Not in and of itself. Enormous good has come from this evolution.

The challenge is the complete disconnect between the expectations of the investor and the completely distant consequences of those investments.

When the distance between the investor and the investment becomes too great, any meaningful connection between the two diminishes or becomes nonexistent. Without any connection, the only relationship left is about the return itself.

> The challenge is the complete disconnect between the expectations of the investor and the completely distant consequences of those investments.

The solution isn't to undo the evolution of mutual funds, but to engage a rudder to guide it. This rudder of core values makes the distance between the investor and investment less of a concern.

This will take a movement of courageous leadership and a bold change in investor expectations. That movement will embrace the courage to lead with the most untapped and impactful strategy available to any leader of any organization. It will be a movement of leaders and investors who not only value defined core values, but who demand that those values be lived. By creating this movement, we can redeem all that makes capitalism good, and in the process, we may just save it.

*   *   *

The overwhelming nature of having to face reality may bring forth the greatest dilemma of all—feeling powerless to change any of it. Yet, sometimes we need to feel overwhelmed to recognize what's bigger than we are. To know there is no overnight solution. To know it is going to require real leadership. To know that beyond leadership it is about legacy.

Leaders can't immediately change what seems bigger than they are. But they can change themselves . . . which in turn changes others. And so it begins.

I realize that any single dilemma I have noted may seem like a significant undertaking for any leader. Pooling them together might feel overwhelming or even impossible to address. A simple awareness makes for a great starting point. It's not only a great place to start. It's a critical backdrop to understand.

> **Leaders can't immediately change what seems bigger than they are. But they can change themselves . . . which in turn changes others. And so it begins.**

2

Discovering the Drift

We don't go running away from our values,
we go drifting away. And one day we wake up
in a place we never meant to be, drifting in a
direction we never would have chosen.

I wrote the words above at a table in a Starbucks while writing my book *Good to the Core*. I had no idea they would become the most called-out words of the book, although I suppose I should have sensed it just from my own life's journey. Those words may well express the greatest dilemma of all. I'm certain that when an organization or a person implodes, it is due to drift.

I was recently asked by a friend to speak to his leadership class of eighth-grade boys. It wasn't my typical corporate audience of executives, and so I was a bit apprehensive whether these middle school students would find my message on core values interesting or relevant. I wasn't prepared for the depth of their engagement or for the wisdom of one particular student in the closing question/answer session. He posed a thoughtful and brilliant question to which I was certain he had already figured out the answer. He asked, "Mr. Blumberg, do you think other people see you drifting before you see it yourself?"

I would urge every leader to remember his question. I think we all know the answer.

Subtle Steps

If only it were one obvious step from good to bad or from right to wrong, there would be so much less heartbreak. Tragedy would be the exception. Financial disasters wouldn't be explained away as acts of incremental deceit or the erosion of character. The decisions we face would seem more like jumping off a cliff than slowly sliding down a slippery slope. Cliffs are more obvious, and executives are much less likely to make an irresponsible jump than they are to begin a treacherous slide.

[Getting from Good to Bad]

Show me a corporation, association, politician, athletic program, religious institution, or marriage where there has been an implosion, and I will show you where there has been a breakdown at the core. And it didn't happen overnight. It happened over time.

It's surprising when it happens, especially when the apex of the problem rests on the shoulders of smart, experienced, successful people. In most cases, it rests with people who have worked incredibly hard to arrive at what is at once the height of their success and the precipice of their fall.

> The student asked, "Mr. Blumberg, do you think other people see you drifting before you see it yourself?"

I don't know about you, but I just don't run into that many people (including leaders at every level) who say they *don't* want to operate from a set of core values. How then do we have so many breakdowns at the core with all of these good people at the helm?

Growing up, one of my favorite singing groups was always hanging out up on the roof, or under the boardwalk, or creating some magic moment! The songs of *the Drifters* bring back a rush of memories. If only I could sing . . . it sure would have been fun to be a *Drifter*. Well, at least that kind of drifter!

But we are far more likely to become a drifter of a different sort. As I wrote during that afternoon in Starbucks, I stumbled upon the logical answer as to why we continue to experience so many organizational implosions: "We don't go running away from our values. We go drifting away. And one day we wake up in a place we never meant to be, drifting in a direction we never would have chosen."

I first realized how much it resonated with people when they came up to visit following my keynote presentations. They would look me in the eye and say, "It's the drift, isn't it?" It never really felt as if they were asking me or telling me. It was as if they simply needed to say it as a repeated reminder and reinforcement for themselves. It wasn't unfamiliar to them. In fact, it was quite familiar, since most had certainly experienced it personally, including me. Many had probably known it since the eighth grade! They just needed to name it. Fully realize it. And, ultimately, they needed to open their eyes to the danger of how something so simple, so subtle, could lead down a road to something so tragic.

> They would look me in the eye and say, "It's the drift, isn't it?"

Their focus and reflection on that simple quote was fortunate. The drift may be the most dangerous dilemma of them all. The drift is so subtle. And subtle is hard to detect; it's all but invisible. It's not necessarily invisible to others, but it's invisible to us. Everyone is vulnerable to the drift. It creates a huge dilemma.

[Knowing When You Left]

After a presentation at the University of Alabama, a participant who had her own version of focusing on the drift approached me and posed her rhetorical question: "If you don't know where you started, how in the world would you ever know you had left?"

That is precisely the value of intentionally knowing your core values. Knowing your core values doesn't prevent you from drifting. In fact, you can pretty much be sure you will drift with daily demands, demanding relationships, and the reality of your humanity. But if you know where you started, *you will know when you have left*. When you start to drift, knowing your core values will let you know you have left your core. That knowledge opens your eyes, heart, and soul to the fact that the drift has begun. Your core values are like a microscope magnifying what is invisible to the naked eye.

> If you don't know where you started, how in the world would you ever know you had left?

The path to bad choices and behaviors is typically not a short one. It is a seductively incremental, likely undetectable pathway paved with some magnetic temptations. It serves us well to know the very moment we leave. That is your magic moment!

[The Little Things]

The challenge with drift is that it always wedges itself into the little things. Just like water, it will find the path of least resistance. The drift rarely begins with a major decision. It creeps its way into the most seemingly insignificant, simple daily decisions. It comes when we are in a rush, when bigger things are pressing. It never starts with a major decision—it just ends with one. A really bad one.

I think we would be shocked to see how many little decisions made each day would be able to trigger drift. Consciously noticing each of these decisions would be virtually impossible. It would take incredible energy and might ultimately drive you crazy.

It isn't about paying attention to each and every decision. It's about investing in what automatically informs those decisions for you, whether those decisions are personal or organizational.

Momentum derived from the little decisions you make often informs the bigger decisions that demand your attention. The issue is what informs the little decisions. The little things *are* the big things. In Chapter 10, you'll see how building value with core values is a daily investment.

Blind Passion

Passion is truly a gift, but when it comes to blind spots it can also be a curse. This is one explanation of why lapses in the judgment of others seem so clear to those on the outside looking in and why we are so quick to ask, "What were they thinking?"

I always hesitate to focus on a specific tragedy when it comes to core values. The fact is that truth is never exactly what it appears to be to the outside world. And the truth is rarely as clear to you on the inside as you would think it would be, especially when you are caught up in something you are really passionate about.

This is particularly true when it comes to the passion of athletics. While sports create endless possibilities for personal development, they can also become an arena of runaway passion and blind loyalty. The same is true when we are experiencing individual or collective success, or are accumulating the almighty dollar. Rather than judging others, we are far better served learning from their heartbreaking examples when it comes to understanding our own potential vulnerabilities. While it is sometimes difficult to relate to examples that seem extreme, they can still be a powerful wake-up call about our own less extreme circumstances—or perhaps a fair warning that something unique to us, maybe not so subtle or small, is approaching on our horizon.

There are times when the alarm in our life is silent, and other times when it is screaming for our attention. The sexual misconduct that seems to have transpired within the otherwise honorable Penn State football program is a heartbreaking example of a screaming alarm.

I don't know exactly what transpired at Penn State. I must admit that my first (and second and third) reaction was to question how so many good people could have missed or ignored something so evil. It is easy to rush to judgment, because hindsight is always 20/20.

It is also much easier to see that evil if you couldn't care less about Penn State football or anything else about Penn State. Everything is always clearer when you are 100 percent objective and have nothing at stake . . . when you have no price to pay for seeing things exactly as they are.

Rather than spending our time casting judgment on the Penn State story, I believe we would be better served pondering the lessons it provides about the blindness of passion and the silent alarms in our own lives.

Passion can blind us to the alarms ringing in our life. If you don't think you have any alarms, you have, by definition, just discovered your first one. We all have alarms, and some are signaling worse dangers than others.

I'm more convinced than ever that *organizational* core values are important, but they will never substitute or replace the cardinal need for well-defined *personal* core values. Organizational core values give us a framework for thought and behavior. Personal core values give us courage in the moment—regardless of the cost. The more clearly we understand the specifics of our personal values, the deeper our courage is likely to run. The Penn State football program's "Success with Honor" was a well-known organizational core value. It was a definition of the professed culture. But it, like any other organizational value, is only as valuable as the connection and commitment it has to our individual personal cores.

Personal values are anything but personal. They are *systemic*—and so is the shrapnel from them when something goes wrong. We depend on one another to have personal core values, to know them, and to live them. Personal and organizational core values are a must, and leaders of any type of organization who are not clear about this imperative are playing an organizational version of Russian roulette.

New York Times writer David Brooks once asked an important question on *Meet the Press*: "Have we lost our sense of right from wrong?" It is a powerful question to ponder. Its answer can become a stark reality if you are winging your personal or organizational values. The hard part about having core values is the fact that they will certainly cost you. The hard part of not knowing your core values is the ultimate truth that the absence of them will eventually destroy you. It is just a matter of time.

Things can be difficult even when you're grounded at your core. In the Penn State case, it was reported that a graduate assistant coach caught a former coach—the defensive coordinator, no less—in the lockerroom shower, engaged in inappropriate actions. Can you imagine stumbling upon one of your heroes in the midst of the unimaginable?

> The hard part of not knowing your core values is the ultimate truth that the absence of them will eventually destroy you.

I can't imagine the shock to your entire system and the complete numbness likely to follow. And yes, that kind of shock can blind you. I'm not talking about when we are on the outside looking in. I'm talking about when you are the one standing in the doorway to the shower.

It is heartbreaking from every angle imaginable, and the only thing that allows you to open your eyes and see the truth is the clearly defined values at your core. And even then, facing the truth can be almost unbearable. Many people on the outside looking in say they're confident that they would have taken every appropriate action in that circumstance— would have gone to the ends of the earth if necessary. But the truth is, they can't know that for sure, because they weren't the one standing in the doorway to the shower.

About the time I was beginning to write this book, I had the opportunity

to meet up with Jerry Porras, coauthor with Jim Collins of *Built to Last.*
We were talking about values, and Jerry said, "We truly understand our
core values when they are put to the test." I believe he is right on target. I
also believe the moment of the test is a really horrible time to start figuring
them out. He agreed.

There are always numerous lessons we can learn from the tragedy of
others if we choose to reflect and learn rather than judge. No matter the
nuance of every detail of the truth, it appears many things went terribly
wrong at Penn State. They really needed to take a close look deep inside
their core.

As do all the rest of us.

[Well-Fueled Passion]

Like all things, passion can have its dark side. We can get caught up in the
momentum that our passion creates. It's been spoken about in numerous
ways. I like to think about it in terms of the old wisdom of see no evil,
hear no evil, speak no evil.

In our world of spin, we can be duped into believing the deceit because
this is where our passion, void of intentional core values, nurtures our
own deceit. It has its own lock on the concept of drift, and it eventually
has its own lock on us. You could describe this as the ends justifying the
means. But it's a bit different than that. The ends justifying the means is
a bit of an intentional justification. This is more subtle and fully unintentional. Much like the drift—you are blinded to its
tightening grip.

Values are the thermostat that shuts down all systems when passion begins to overheat.

Values must precede passion. Otherwise, passion
can curdle values into poison. Where core values
precede passion, they are woven into the substance
of the passion. Our passion must be fueled and
guided by our core values.

Our passion is a beautiful thing when fueled

from a well-defined core. Values are the thermostat that shuts down all systems when passion begins to overheat. Otherwise passion becomes opaque within us and can eventually create a blind spot in all we see, and eventually in all we don't see.

[Coping Mechanism]

Sometimes our blind spots can become our convenient coping mechanism. It's not that we can't see; it's that we choose not to see. In some cases, we look away, and in others we simply choose not to open our eyes.

This often happens when we have a great position. A position we don't want to lose. This can be in the form of a title, community stature, or even broader notoriety, income, or perceived self-worth.

Blind spots can serve as a nerve block. We eventually recognize this and simply choose to accept it as part of life. We can learn to justify anything if it helps us cope day to day, month to month, and sometimes year to year. In fact, the longer it goes on, the easier the medicine goes down.

It could be technically defined as plausible deniability. You know. I know. And ultimately we all know we all know—but we all pretend we really don't know!

Without core values, the medicine settles quite nicely in your stomach. It is only when core values are nurtured in your gut that you have any chance to eject this toxic medicine.

[Perception Deception]

The morning following the only vice presidential debate of the 2012 presidential election, my good friend Dr. Beverly Ann Smallwood made an observation in a Facebook posting. She simply noted the irony in how millions could watch the same exact event and see such different things. How? Perception, she noted. There is no question that perception is a powerful force.

Perception can also be a deceptive force.

Perception stems from perspective, and perspective is often driven by our circumstances. Our circumstances certainly can alter what we see and how we feel. They can lead us to some factual conclusions about our experience and to some unfounded assumptions too.

Not to oversimplify, but I often think about how the temperature on any given day can be a great indicator of my theory. A 45-degree day is factually a 45-degree day no matter what day it falls on. Let's assume one of those days falls in early autumn and the other one in the middle of winter. Factually, the temperature is exactly the same, assuming winds and humidity are the same. But what we actually experience can be significantly different. It is our circumstances (e.g., our typical experience of early fall temperatures or the biting cold of the dead of winter) that define our perspective and can therefore create completely different perceptions of the exact same temperature. The 45-degree autumn day may feel downright cold, while the 45-degree winter day can embrace us with a sense of warmth. The same set of facts viewed from a different perspective can create a completely different perception.

This truth doesn't only apply to temperatures. If it goes unnoticed, it can prove fatal to leaders—especially leaders without a well-defined core. The problem is that sometimes it is so unnoticeable . . . unless we are consciously aware that perception deception is continually in play. And every leader needs a strategic counterattack to diminish the blinding capability of this deception.

Sometimes this deception can be fed from the outside, when we surround ourselves only with people who think like we do and have precisely the same viewpoints—whether on business strategy, politics, spiritual practices, or theological beliefs. When you never have a counterpoint, you can rest assured it's only a matter of time until you are well on your way to drifting toward the deception of your own perception.

As the pressures on business performance become increasingly focused on the short term, business leaders fall into the trap of this deception. As our political rhetoric becomes louder and more divisive, politicians and citizens fall into the trap of this deception. It can happen in religious circles where we become so arrogant that we believe our human mind has fully understood the ways of an eternal God. And the more intense the perception deception becomes, the louder we shout our viewpoint.

From there, it becomes a vicious spiral downward into a greater deception because there's no one with other viewpoints. We have repelled every one of them! In doing so, we create our own isolation. Every leader needs to be fed with counterpoints. These viewpoints don't have to change our stance, but they do need to test our perception. More often than not, they will fine-tune our stance.

The counterpoint is a useful outside force. Our core values are a powerful inside force.

The way to easily see the impact of circumstances is to realize how quickly we see a value disconnect in others. We are not in their circumstances. We don't share their blind spots. We can, therefore, see the drift in motion.

I'm certain you have experienced this. You look at the missteps of a leader in the midst of great success and shake your head. You wonder how in the world they got into those circumstances. You wonder how they could not have seen it coming. It's so clear to you, and you are not even familiar with the details . . . which is precisely why you *can* so easily see it!

You can't prevent the drift, but you can minimize its destructive potential. You can take advantage of the vantage points from where others see you. So easy to see for others . . . so hard to see for ourselves.

Anchors

Boats are equipped with anchors for a reason. Anchors become increasingly valuable in a storm. And so do our core values. Like an anchor on board, our core values slow us down when we have inevitably started to drift! They are our drift busters.

[A Steady Hold]

Leaders and captains both have a guaranteed potential for drift. The environmental conditions of a storm—whether sudden or predicted—create a known dilemma for the captain of the ship and the leader of an organization. The anchor is on the boat in anticipation of the storm; likewise, values need to be in our core with the same thoughtful anticipation.

I think we would all agree that being in the middle of a storm is a really bad time to realize you should have brought along an anchor. Likewise, being in the middle of an organizational crisis is a really bad time to realize you should have developed a meaningful set of core values. There's one major difference between an anchor and your core values. An anchor is a critical resource in the midst of a storm; core values are a strategic resource to navigate you away from a storm in the first place. Yet, if a storm comes upon you, a set of core values, committed to long before, will steady your ship through the rough waters.

[Lifeguards]

As powerful as the anchoring with core values may be, it is not enough. We were designed to need others, and this is surely the case when it comes to the drift. While our values will help us sense the drift, other people are likely to help us see it.

We generally want people who *get* our drift. Have you ever been trying to explain a complicated idea to someone (or even a simple, obvious idea) and in frustration just ask them, "Do you get my drift?" Meaning, "Do you understand me?" That's what we want!

When it comes to drifting, *we need people who catch our drift and bring us back!* You might think of them as your lifeguard, or better yet, as your Drift Catcher! All of us need Drift Catchers, and we need to proactively seek them out. These are people who love you enough to tell you the truth, and whom you love enough to listen to—even when you don't like what they're telling you. This is especially critical for top leaders.

Effective leaders specifically seek out their Drift Catchers. Drift Catchers are people you completely trust. You literally give your Drift Catchers your list of core values (personal and organizational). You also give them permission to call you out when they see you drifting from your core.

When they honor your request, you don't explain away the divergence. You embrace the alarm they are sounding for you and simply say thank you.

In doing the hard work of defining your core and enlisting others to guide you, you don't eliminate the drift but you eliminate its grip on you.

* * *

Drifting may be the greatest challenge of all. Much of what I have previously set forth about the difficulties facing leaders comes from forces on the outside. It's critical to maintain an awareness of these outside forces, as they can have a strong impact—a magnetic pull that's hard to resist and that subtly starts the drift. Yet, ultimately, the anchor is within us. It's the precise awareness of our own core values.

3

Carrying the Lead
in Leadership

Some things can be led solely by the example in how they are lived.
Core values are one of them. They are leadership's greatest call . . . and
heaviest burden. There is, indeed, a "lead" in leadership. This "lead" is
pronounced like a heavy weight . . . phonetically spelled "led." It's in a
willingness to carry this weight that a leader holds the potential to lead.

With the market's plethora of books on leadership, you would think everyone wants to be a leader. While many may want to be a leader, unfortunately only a few really want to lead. That is, only a few want to actually carry the lead (the heavy weight) of leadership.

There is a long-standing question in leadership circles: Are leaders born or made? I think the authors of leadership books are hoping they are made—otherwise, what would be the point of writing about leadership? I have always answered this long-standing question with one word: both!

The larger question might well be, *Is someone in a leadership position willing to personally carry the weight of leadership?* The weight doesn't care if you are a born leader or a leader made along the way. The real question should be, *Are you willing to actually carry the "lead" of leadership?* Not direct. Not manage. Not reap the benefits of a sought-after position. But are you willing to dig deep to find the real potential of your leadership regardless of your position? It seems so basic. I would suggest it is much harder than it looks, at least at first.

Leading Is about . . . Leading

The need for a leadership mind-set can arise at any moment and at any level within an organization. I believe this is why the market for leadership books blossomed over the past two decades. Organizations were becoming much larger and far more complex. The speed of change inside and out was accelerating. Even smaller organizations were seeking leadership insight for those in key positions.

The problem is that we have chosen to focus on almost every aspect of leadership except for the most impactful and untapped of all of them—the very core of the leader and the organization they lead.

Everyone has the potential to bring leadership wisdom to their work regardless of the level of their position. And many do. I have often said that leadership is not about a position. Yet, sometimes a position will demand your leadership. Followers who are in positions of leadership generally don't create a Return On Integrity. They often create a drain on integrity.

[Leaderless Leadership]

There is no single factor or circumstance that will undermine core values—and therefore your Return On Integrity—more than the issue of leaderless leadership. Leadership is about leading. Period. Leaders go first. And nothing could ring more true when it comes to core values.

It is easy to find examples of followers in leadership positions in an organization. And when we do, we find leaderless leadership. When it comes down to developing value with core values, they pretty quickly reveal themselves. It boils down to their one predictable question: "Can you show me examples of other organizations that have created value by being strategic with core values?"

I get the value in having points of data, but I'm convinced that most aren't really looking for points of data. Some are looking for comfort rather than embracing their responsibility to lead. Others are looking for an excuse to avoid the most demanding aspect of their leadership.

This is precisely what followers do. They look for proof of where something has already been done, and then they *follow* that example. That might work in directing initiatives or the latest fad of priorities of organizational leadership, but it simply doesn't work when it comes to leading from your core.

Leaders find the courage to create the examples that followers in leadership positions will eventually point to and then try to follow. But in following others, they never really lead. They simply put on the veneer of leadership and get in the parade to follow another. Unfortunately, oftentimes they are in a parade led by a leaderless leader, and so their drift begins.

Real leaders do the hard work to look to only one place . . . deep within. It is from there that they not only fuel their leadership—they define it.

So what's the leadership dilemma? There isn't one for a leaderless leader because they aren't actually leading. The dilemma is only for an actual leader; they actually have to live from their core. It is the only way they lead.

Of course, it's easier said than done. It's a heavy load of lead. It's a dilemma that every leader must learn to carry.

[You First . . . Then Others]

There is a critical element of leadership that calls upon your ability to inspire others to get something done. The art of appropriate and responsible delegation is at its finest in these cases.

Nothing could be more inappropriate or irresponsible than delegation when it comes to core values. It starts with the leader. And this is what makes building value with core values such a formidable task. You must first fully embrace it yourself. You must know it, own it, live it, and hold yourself deeply accountable for it. It is the only way you can lead it. In other words, this isn't something you can get others to do by delegating it. It's impossible. It will never gain traction. The old "Do as I say and not as I do" simply won't work.

Therein resides the beauty of leading the Return On Integrity. You must first lead yourself before you can lead others. It has been said that *if you can lead one you can lead many, but if you can't lead one you can't lead any.* The one, of course, is you. This could easily be the mantra in leading a Return On Integrity!

The formula is simply that easy and therefore so hard. When it comes to the strategy of core values, it all begins with you. Leading it is living it. There is no other option. It's a leader's only choice. Are you willing to learn it, live it, and eventually leverage it to lead it? You have to become the poster child, the living example. This is not about doing unto others as you would have them do unto you. You can only expect from others what you have already been willing to expect from yourself.

Monkey See . . . Monkey Do

If followers were not so good at watching, a leader could dictate rather than lead. It might have impact but little potential. Followers can be good at judging and are even better at mimicking what they see. If they see their leader's core is an inch deep and a mile wide, they will develop a core—you guessed it—an inch deep and a mile wide.

I was watching as I began my career, and I trust you were too. I remember after joining Arthur Andersen, I was assigned to the Federal Express audit. Pam was the senior auditor. She was exceptional in leading our team. I watched what she did and how she did it. In those first few weeks, I only hoped I would be as good as Pam if I were promoted to her level. My watchful eye would continue throughout my career.

We forget that in at least one way, leadership is monkey business.

[Everyone Is Watching]

My biggest fear for leaders is that they will forget how much they used to watch others in the earliest days of their career. We tend to lose perspective or lose touch with those memories. Today's leaders work under such competing and complex demands that they simply don't realize just how much others are watching their every move, listening to their every word. They no longer realize the impact they have on all who follow.

The great inconvenience of leadership is the fact that everyone is watching. They are watching consciously and subconsciously. What they see and don't see matters, and it matters a lot!

I'm not talking about the surface-level behaviors. Sure, those are important, and we will address those. But followers are far more sophisticated than that.

> **We forget that in at least one way, leadership is monkey business.**

A leader can't lose sight of this simple principle. It has to be an ongoing part of their conscious leadership each and every day. Without everyday awareness, a leader soon loses sight of those watchful eyes. Yet, their impact still touches all those who are watching.

Remember . . . if you can lead one, you can lead many. If you can't lead one, you can't lead any. The heavy lifting of leadership begins with you. Otherwise, you are not leading. Yet, you are still having an impact beacause followers don't only watch. They follow.

[Imitation]

In recent decades, students of human nature and behavior have noted the reality of imitation. But it doesn't take a scientist to explain this natural phenomenon. I think most of us can look back on our experiences and see numerous examples of when we imitated others or when others imitated us. Think about our early years of childhood and our years in school.

The stronger the connection between two individuals, the more imitation is likely to happen in a significant way. In many cases, it often begins without notice.

You can initially see it in superficial ways. Have you ever met someone who has unique characteristics, behaviors, or vocabulary? If it is someone you quickly and naturally connected with, it is likely you found yourself picking up some of those characteristics. If you didn't notice, it is likely others around you did!

This imitation is quite natural. Some have tried to use it in manipulative ways to create a temporary connection. It's taught in sales courses, where it's referred to as mirroring and pacing. It involves creating an imitation of someone else so you can connect with that person in order to make a sale. There may be some proof that a buyer will fall for this, but I doubt it creates lasting relationships or repeat sales.

> **Remember . . . if you can lead one, you can lead many. If you can't lead one, you can't lead any. The heavy lifting of leadership begins with you. Otherwise, you are not leading. Yet, you are still having an impact because followers don't only watch. They follow.**

While such tactics make for poor leadership, they do reinforce the power of imitation even in artificial short-term interventions. In the case of followers, it may not be that they like you, it may simply be that they have to report to you. And they will ultimately imitate what they see.

Paradox of Leadership

The concept of paradox is fascinating to me. Not too far from my home, there was a neighborhood road that ended in an intersection of a well-traveled street. There was a stop sign that evidently wasn't effective enough to prevent accidents. Beneath that stop sign, the city added an additional sign, formally printed in black letters on a white background, that simply read *Look Again*.

That is the gift of a paradox. It beckons you to *look again*. And so it is with leadership. Paradox celebrates the underlying truth of what would appear to be contradictory on the surface. Some examples might include the following:

- Each end is a beginning, and each beginning is the start to an end.
- You can find great joy in the midst of deep sorrow.
- Making no decision is a decision.
- The faster I go, the more behind I get.
- The more things change, the more they stay the same.
- You must let go of a relationship to be able to hold on to it.
- The need to control is controlling.
- In giving, we receive.
- We fix others best by fixing ourselves.
- You can be surrounded by many, while still being lonely.
- Saying yes to one thing likely means saying no to another.
- You can obtain more by having less.
- The less you need, the more you have.
- Silence speaks volumes.
- Perfection is imperfect.
- Laughter can bring tears to your eyes.
- The day you think you have all the answers is the day you don't understand the question!

- Buddha found enlightenment when he quit seeking it.
- The same is not always equal.

One of my favorite paradoxes in leadership is noted in the book *Management of the Absurd* by Richard Farson: *"Every great strength is a great weakness."* I have often thought of it in terms that every weakness can usually be traced to a strength overplayed. A paradox indeed.

The Bible is full of paradox. Some samples would include the following:

- "But many who are first will be last, and the last first." (Mark 10:31)
- "The greatest among you will be your servant." (Matthew 23:11)
- "If I must boast, I will boast of the things that show my weakness." (2 Corinthians 11:30)
- "For those who exalt themselves will be humbled, and those who humble themselves will be exalted." (Matthew 23:12)
- "When pride comes, then comes disgrace, but with humility comes wisdom." (Proverbs 11:2)

It's interesting how many have to do with humility and vulnerability. It's a paradoxical leadership lesson within itself. Paradox encourages us to not only look again but also to look around, underneath, and upside down. It's also an essential element of leadership and an insightful resource when leaders become students of their own core.

[Servant Leadership]

Servant leadership is not a new idea. Yet, it is a refreshing one that has found new wind in its sails over the past two decades. Consultants have promoted it and executive coaches have helped leaders develop an understanding of it.

It is a leadership paradox. It holds the framework for a leader's success. It isn't a mind-set that has been practiced by many leaders—only the great ones, the ones whose leadership impact long outlasted their time in their position.

Many leaders might sincerely consider themselves to be a servant leader. They may consciously try to form their behaviors into the look and feel of a servant leader. They may even have a heart that is engaged and ready to serve. Their followers may experience them as a servant leader. However, the greatest paradox may be that these leaders are not aware of the values at their own core, and they may not intentionally be leading from the values at the core of their organization. This disconnect can certainly weigh down the very best servant leader.

[Highly Visible, Yet Isolated and Insulated]

Another paradox we should address is how a very visible leader can experience isolation and insulation. This isolation and insulation is not apparent to anyone they lead, and sometimes isn't even apparent to the leaders themselves.

It's a subtle reality that eventually catches a leader by surprise. It can show up in many ways. Feeling special, unique, and responsible can initially be seductive. But these opaque veneers can wear thin and reveal the lack of authentic conversation and genuine friendship. Regardless of their position, leaders are never above basic human needs. As leaders gain in stature and importance, the greater number of people they have around them can actually lead to a declining number of *real* friendships.

It's a paradox so important that if left unnoticed and unattended, it will diminish a leader's effectiveness or ultimately bring them down.

Fear Pressure

Over the years, "consultant speak" used a question as a probe for business risks or vulnerabilities facing an executive: "What keeps you up at night?" While asked figuratively, I'm sure it was also meant literally. Another, more straightforward way to ask the question would be, *What are you afraid of?*

I think we can easily see the "drifting" effects of peer pressure. They are just as real when it comes to fear pressure! And sometimes what we really fear may just surprise us—and significantly impact the effectiveness of our leadership.

Conventional wisdom suggests the most common fear named by the average person is the fear of public speaking. The same conventional wisdom indicates that the fear of public speaking ranks even above death. *Really?*

Having given hundreds of presentations, I naturally have a hard time relating to that statistic, as would most leaders. There are a number of leaders who are not afraid of public speaking, but they simply don't like it and haven't invested the time, effort, or commitment that their leadership platform deserves. Public speaking has become a critical leadership skill. It is also a skill that will be critical in leading others to their core. But I digress . . . we'll get back to that later. At least a leader's reservation about public speaking is one of those fears that becomes readily apparent to the leader and usually to others. Other fears are not that straightforward. It's an important question for every leader: *What am I afraid of?*

[Fear of Failure]

Public speaking isn't the only element that might be causing unsuspecting fear pressure. Another fear that few leaders might admit, but many might experience, is the fear of failure.

Countless participants, in audiences from coast to coast, have shared their fear of failure with me following one of my presentations. I appreciate their honesty and am grateful for their awareness. All leaders would be well served to assess this fear in themselves. Not acknowledging it can have significant implications in the day-to-day perspectives and behaviors of any leader.

> **Are you playing to win—or playing not to lose?**

My great friend, mentor, and leadership expert Kevin Freiberg first drew my attention to this powerful question: Are you playing to win—or playing not to lose?

Fear of failure will always put you in a defensive posture of playing *not to lose*. It is a weak, and frankly boring, brand of leadership.

While playing not to lose may sound like a conservative approach to leadership, it may very well be a deceptive wedge edging its way between a leader and their core. The different slant on that great question may be—are you playing or are you leading?

[Fear of Success]

Fear of failure can create quite a dilemma for any leader. So can the fear of success.

Success can create its own demands. Henry Kissinger, the fifty-sixth US secretary of state, put it this way: Each success only buys you a ticket to a more difficult problem!

This is true. Few leaders escape the incremental demand of continued success. The increasing demand could be the most conscious or subconscious fear of all. Most leaders won't necessarily see it as a fear of success, but they will likely feel the fear of the demands success brings. The increasing demands can bring the dawning of a drift from their core.

> **Each success only buys you a ticket to a more difficult problem!**

Intentionally trying to eliminate fear can be a tall order. A leader's willingness to embrace their core can eventually make the fear irrelevant. You might say it is one of the Returns On Integrity.

Too Much to Lose

If there is one thing a leader should fear about success, it's all the trappings that come with it. If there is anything that can incrementally undermine a leader, it's the eventual arrival in a place called "Too Much to Lose." It's a sticky place to be, because a lot of things tend to stick to you—or you tend to attach to them.

[Attachments]

As leaders attain "success," they can have a tendency to "attach" to anything and sometimes everything—especially things like wealth, power, accessibility to other successful people, interesting experiences, adventurous opportunities, or whatever other whimsical opportunities that may come along. Sometimes attachments are not things at all. On the surface, attachments can seem beneficial. They can even come packaged in what appear to be noble things, such as commitment, passion, and reliability. Woven behind such a noble facade as these, they can be hard to detect.

Our attachments are another paradox. When you are clinging to something, you are forcing it to stay put, rather than trusting it will be with you for as long as it is the right thing for you. In other words, if you're forcing it, it's not real or healthy. These rewards of the position can become traps within the position. Sometimes what we hang on to in turn begins to cling to us. Unchecked, these things can eventually become addictions. And addictions are the fuel for drift.

> **Our attachments are another paradox.**

Values are different than the trappings of attachments. Grabbing values is like trying to grab air or water. You can be in them, absorb them, and certainly benefit from them . . . but you can't just attach yourself to them.

Perhaps a leader's best shot at remaining connected to their core is to embrace the practice of detachment to the trappings of success. The thing you attach to is not the problem. It is the attachment to it that begins to change the relationship you have with the trappings. At some point you no longer own them—they own you and the core within you.

The moment you attach to something, you have something to lose. We all do it to some degree. It eventually becomes a problem when you feel like you have too much to lose.

By the time you realize it, you have drifted a long way from your core. As attachments cling to you, they pull you in whatever direction they need to go and you simply follow, serving them in any way that keeps you connected to them. By that point, you have arrived at a place you never meant to be, drifting in a direction you never would have chosen.

[Self-Identity]

Our social context and norms of behavior can set the stage for this potential attachment. When was the last time you were at a social event and meeting someone for the first time when they asked, "*Who* are you?" It's likely you haven't posed that question to others when meeting them for the first time either. The question usually posed is *So, what do you do?* We are not used to the *who* question. It might initially lead to a response of "Huh?" before evolving into a far more interesting conversation.

But once you are in a leadership role, the "what" question may never be asked of you, because the answer is already known, or expected to be known. It's part of how others identify you. It can come with the territory. But what people really yearn to know is *who* you are. Don't worry, they will never ask. They will just watch.

As a leader, the problem comes when your self-identity is attached to the "what" rather than defined by the "who." Brands, logos, and slogans might go a long way in corporate or organizational identity, but they make for lethal recipes when it comes to a leader's self-identity—or anyone else's identity, for that matter.

A leader's identity placed anywhere other than within their core is a pathway to attachment. It's a setup for something to lose. A leader who doesn't intentionally and consciously know their own core will find their self-identity in *something* outside their core, and most likely, they will attach themselves to it.

A leader who doesn't intentionally and consciously know and lead the core of an organization will find the organization's self-identity in other measurements, and so will every other leader, manager, and employee within it. This not only gets in the way of our relationship with ourselves, it certainly influences our relationship with others too.

[Relationships]

We are social beings; relationships matter. For leaders, relationships can get complicated. Sometimes it's because of the motives behind the relationship others have with them. Other times it's because a leader thinks a relationship exists because of who they are, when oftentimes it exists solely because of what they are. Relationships matter, and leaders' intentional connections to their own core determine the substance of their relationships.

The true quality of a leader's relationships can be determined by who is still around after they are no longer in that leadership position. Many leaders have seen those relationships evaporate following their own firing, merger, layoff, or retirement.

The depth of a leader's connection to their own core directly correlates to the depth and quality of the relationships they will experience while they're in a position of leadership, and when they're eventually out of it.

When leaders aren't connected to their own core, the foundation of most of their relationships is tied to their position. These relationships become a conditional attachment. Keeping the relationships becomes conditional to keeping the position. Relationships matter, and these relationships can be a lot to lose—or at least they seem to be.

[Income and Stability]

Addictions come in many shapes and sizes. In some cases, addictions can happen almost overnight. Some forms of substance abuse fall into this category. Other addictions subtly happen over time. And sometimes our attachment to one of these addictions can alter our perception of reality. So it goes with income and stability.

If leaders don't understand their core, it is easy for income and stability to become not only all about what they have but also the lens through which they define who they are.

It is easy to become attached to a level of income, and it is easy for income to become attached to your perception of stability. In the absence of a leader's connection to their core, income and stability become welded together. And when they do, it can weigh down your leadership and become a heavy load for any leader to carry.

[A Theology . . . of Your Own]

For some, a level of maturity is defined as arriving in a place where you realize you don't have all the answers—and that you don't need to. Often, leaders can fall into the trap of not only thinking they have all the right answers but of developing their own theology.

Typically, we think of theology in the arena of religion. It's a good arena to look for this particular example. A tight grip on a theology can lead you to thinking you have all the answers. I have always shuddered at our audacity to believe we have fully grasped the complete understanding of the God of our universe in such a way that we would be in a position to have all the answers. Believing we have all the right answers or preaching as if we do can create a viewpoint that can blind us to the truth. It can create an addiction to the need to always be right. That sense of "being the one who is right" can seem like a lot to lose.

Theology isn't exclusive to the hallways of religious institutions. Leaders of secular organizations can fall into the same trap of developing their own theology of having all the right answers and making a religion of their entire experience. Rarely do these leaders come from being intentionally grounded in their core, but they are often attached to many things. Usually, they have a lot to lose, starting with their own theology.

The problem of "too much to lose" rests in the fact that it can be so hard to see. Rarely are the things to which we attach, in and of themselves, bad things. It is our clinging attachment that is the problem. If losing what we "have" weighs on us more than the thought of losing our "core," it's just a matter of time until the drift begins.

A leader's core is designed to carry him or her. The values identified inside can carry quite a load, especially when one is not holding on to anything else.

So What's a Leader to Do?

There is a plethora of leadership books filled with ideas, how-tos, must-dos, and yes, theology. But ultimately, it comes down to choice. All of life is a choice, and so is leadership.

It would seem that leading from your core would be natural. It is. But it won't seem that way at first. It will seem quite unnatural—possibly to you, and certainly to others. We will be digging deep, and few have led from such a place as this. So what's a leader to do? *Lead anyway.*

Years ago, we made a big mistake. We created the wrong title. We named it "executive." We came up with another title and called it "officer," which brought a military flavor to the executive suite. Then we decided to blend it all together and created the position of Chief Executive Officer. CEO for short. Brilliant! Yes, brilliant for an emphasis on execution, but not so much for leadership.

Executives execute, but they don't necessarily lead. Maybe we should have titled the position "Leader," or "L" for short. But then again, maybe we should just keep titles out of it altogether. A leader fully connected to his or her core and intentionally intersecting with the values of the organization simply doesn't need a title. They are the title.

The first choice is to embrace the responsibility of leading others, so that those who follow are in a position to execute all that needs to be done. Perhaps if we had more people truly leading from their core, we would decide the position needs an updated title.

When you start leading differently, you are likely to get an earful. That's not to say that a leader shouldn't have an ear for others. But regardless of what they hear, they need to lead anyway. What a leader hears needs to be processed through their ears, but evaluated through their core. No one has ever been well served by a leader who hears, then follows.

So what's a leader do? Lead anyway.

When a leader decides to build value with core values, there is no question that he is going to hear a lot.

So what's a leader to do? Lead anyway.

Some of those voices will come from the typical naysayers who burn all their creativity figuring out why things won't work rather than finding the creative courage to help make them work. A leader will need to lead anyway.

Some of those voices will come from those who realize it will demand meaningful change from them, personally, and they are bankrupt of any currency that requires more than a shallow exchange rate. A leader will need to lead anyway.

Some of those voices will come from those intelligently armed with measurements, yet blind to the valuable wisdom that is not directly measurable. A leader will need to lead anyway.

Some of those voices will come from peers outside the organization in reputable roles as chief executive officers—those who are long on executing, but inept at leading anything or anyone. They will speak with authority, sometimes arrogance, often with argumentative assaults. Few of these voices will come with answers, but will come asking for proof.

That's what followers in leadership positions want, and it's what leaders ultimately create. And so you will need to lead anyway.

Some of these voices you will hear; other voices you won't hear, because they'll be behind your back. Yet, none of these voices will be as dangerous as the silent voice of doubt inside you.

And when the volume of that voice becomes deafeningly loud, you will need to take one more step forward and lead anyway.

In today's world of short-term focus and immediate gratification, it will likely seem to be a long haul. Especially when you are trying to carry the weight of your leadership. Trying to build value with core values. Trying to establish a genuine Return On Integrity. It's a journey where you can only hope to make some meaningful progress across the landscape of your career.

Are you fully ready? Probably not. That's OK. All you have to do is take the next small step. So just keep reading. It isn't about readiness; it's about making the commitment to lead anyway! It's a choice you will never regret.

Section 2:

Definition

E arlier, I mentioned that one of my greatest fears in speaking on the topic of core values is thinking that many participants are going to write off the topic as something they already know all about. Yet, it's interesting that once participants start down the path of thinking beyond the surface level of the topic, the most common question someone will ask is, *So what exactly is a core value?*

It's a surprising question when you think you already know all about it! There isn't a simple answer because when it comes to core values, a concise definition can never explain what your individual journey will help you discover. What's even more surprising (and paradoxical!) is that from that point forward, there will be an ebb and flow between the clearer it gets and the more confusing it becomes—and then in the midst of the confusion, you find an advanced level of clarity.

The good news is that you don't have to have all the answers or even that much clarity to begin digging to your core. Only the process will bring you the unique answers and increased clarity you will need.

4

Defining Core Values

The mission isn't to figure out the definition of core values. The mission is to discover the values at your core. You don't exactly need the former to find the latter. The first is an intellectual exercise, and the second is an emotional awakening.

So, you ask, *What is a core value?*
Typically, when trying to understand something, we start by drawing on a definition from a dictionary or a Google search. I was recently speaking at a lunch-and-learn with a small group of managing partners from law firms. One of the attorneys said, "John, can you give me a specific definition of what exactly is a core value?" He spoke just like a true attorney, and I loved it! Which is why I smiled and simply replied, "I bet you would love that definition, wouldn't you?" He smiled at my jest, as I followed up by saying, "We aren't trying to use our intellectual and creative energy to come up with a definition of core values. We are actually trying to discover the specific values within our

core. As you are in the process of discovering your own core values, you will find what a core value actually is and you won't need a dictionary definition to discover it." It immediately seemed to make a great deal of sense to him.

When it comes to core values, most people don't go that far. Most simply draw on a vague idea or experience of it.

Unfortunately, few of those experiences have gone far enough or deep enough to give them great examples. That's true when leaders rising to the top of organizations search for meaningful examples from predecessors. Some reach back to community organizations with small staffs and multiple volunteers, or to government services, or to churches. Some reach back to the very homes in which they were raised.

In most cases, those searching for the definitions of core values may find solid examples of good behavior (or bad), may find experiences that would make for great classroom case studies to navigate right from wrong, or may draw on the painful lesson of a bad personal choice.

Some may reconnect to an outstanding teachable moment or a parental lecture. Most will likely reach back for a reactive point of data rather than an experience witnessing someone living a purposeful defined, understood, and intentionally lived core. While we want definition, what we need is a discovery.

While we want a definition, what we need is a discovery.

[What Is a Core Value?]

I can point you to several images that may help give a definition to core values. Each might shed a bit of light on your search, but we have to be careful not to oversimplify these very rich resources. Doing so undermines their potential. It is precisely what we've done in the past, and we paid a dear price for it. Our core is not just a thing. It is the essence of who we are.

Our core and our soul could very well be described as two sides of the same coin. If so, it would be a coin that holds great value when well spent.

More pragmatically, we might think of looking at our core like a colorful prism. When we hold it up to the light and slowly turn it, we see endless features. Yet, the longer we look at it, even as we continue to turn it, we begin to see familiar patterns.

Thinking of a kaleidoscope may help you imagine peering into your core. With a kaleidoscope there are a few basic ingredients through which you can see a variety of beautiful designs. Yet, over time the wide variety of designs tend to become familiar.

The process for defining your own core will be as much of an art as it is a science. It is far more complicated, challenging, and refreshing than picking some words from a list on a piece of paper or a few cards from a deck. This process isn't about getting to a quick answer. It's about embarking on an impactful process.

If you personally need to pursue an initial framework to define core values through definitions and descriptions expressed in words, then have at it. Take just a few moments to peruse a favorite dictionary or online resource searching for "core values." I have found a few verbose attempts to put arms around the concept of personal and organizational core values. You may find such definitions helpful.

> The central, innermost, or most essential part . . . of anyone.

After looking to various resources for a core values definition myself, I decided to simply look up the word "core." It seemed more helpful. One simple definition caught my attention: The central, innermost, or most essential part . . . of anything. I think it is helpful for us to simply change the last word to "*anyone.*"

It didn't seem to be so much a definition as an invitation to discover what is central, what is innermost, and what is truly most essential.

Our core values hold so much more depth and potential than can be captured in a word definition. There are no words that do justice to the insights you will eventually experience along the journey of actually discovering them. No definition will ever fully guide or substitute what you will explore, learn, and realize as you start the process of looking for what values reside within your core. You will know them when you see them, and no definition should stand as judge to them. The same is true for the values of the organization you lead.

We would be well served to put our energy into an emotionally engaging search to find the actual values in our core rather than intellectually debating a definition that defines the nature of what values are. As evidenced by almost any dictionary definition, I think we pretty much get the idea. What we don't know are the specifics of what really matters—our *actual* core values.

Our intellectual side wants to know what a core value is. What our emotional side needs to know is which core values are within us.

> In your persistent search for your core values, you actually won't find them! I know that doesn't sound encouraging. The encouraging part is . . . *they will find you.*

It might sound impossible, but let me share a vision and a bit of encouragement for the journey ahead. In your persistent search for your core values, you actually won't find them! I know that doesn't sound encouraging. The encouraging part is . . . *they will find you.* Paradoxically, this won't happen unless you persistently search for them.

I remember, as a young boy, sitting around our family dinner table in Memphis one night. My dad was boasting how my mom had chased him throughout their courting years. Of course, my mom's response brought a different perspective to that time in history. My dad wasn't buying any of that. Then he added a twist I will never forget when he said, "Yep, she chased me until I caught her!" I loved that. I think it is precisely that way in discovering our core values. You will chase them until they catch you. It's worth the chase.

By the way, if you think some great definition will give you the insight to discover the values at your core . . . think again. No matter how robust the definition, you will still be grasping for words—the words that describe your core values. We'll get to those later.

Beyond a definition, a lot of questions still remain as one starts this journey of discovery. So let's explore a few together.

[Why Are the Specifics Important?]

This is a question I'm asked a lot. It's a really good question. Actually, specifics aren't important—*they are essential.* I'm not saying getting there will be easy. I can promise you, at times, it will get frustrating. In fact, it will get so frustrating you will be convinced that specifics aren't only unessential—they are disturbing, distracting, and possibly destructive.

I get a lot of pushback on this idea of specifics. And if you don't want to push back just yet—you will. If this process were easy, more leaders would have gone down this path long ago. We typically don't ignore such useful resources unless it's a really rough road to get there. Getting to specifics makes it all the more challenging.

The conventional wisdom likes to refer to being values-based, as in "I'm a values-based person." That would be true. All of us are values-based. That includes the most evil leaders who have walked this planet. The question is, which values? All of us operate from a values base. Some of us do this consciously, but most do it subconsciously. It's all about selecting intentional values or being guided by unintentional values that have been constructed by needs, wants, and behaviors drifting over time.

To some extent, this makes sense to a lot of leaders until they settle into a more logical pushback. Bringing it to a more conscious level, leaders embrace their own gut feelings or intuition about their core values. It makes for a strong argument. Twenty or thirty years ago, it would have been a convincing argument. I believe twenty to thirty years ago, having a gut feeling or intuition about your core values might have worked quite well. It may be one of the reasons that so many well-intentioned leaders continue to operate from that default perspective.

There's only one problem. In those twenty or thirty years, the world has changed significantly on many fronts. One of those fronts is speed. The speed at which we move, the speed at which change is thrust upon us, the speed at which decisions are made.

Specifics matter.

Specifics matter because at the speed we are moving today, a gut feeling or intuition can be a really risky formula. To make matters worse, we are in *slow motion* compared to where we are headed. The exponential advances in the speed of technology have only gotten started. That's why intentionally discovering our core is more essential and valuable than ever.

Thirtysomething years ago, I was living in Houston. My wife, Cindy, and I had been married for a month. It was in early August 1983, and Hurricane Alicia came off the Gulf and made a direct hit on Houston. I can still picture us looking out the window of our new apartment seeing objects fly by at 125 miles an hour. I'm not sure we should have been looking out a window, but it was interesting to watch. After a while, the heavy rains tapered to a drizzle. The winds calmed and the clouds parted a bit. Cindy and I took the opportunity to go out for a stroll. We returned about 45 minutes later. The dark clouds started gathering again, the breeze became a destructive wind, and the torrential downpours resumed. Then we noticed more things flying by at 125 miles an hour—in the opposite direction. Hurricane Alicia left behind plenty of destruction in its path.

Yet in the eye—in the core—of that powerful storm, there was a real sense of peace and calm. Leaders will face powerful storms along the way. The specifics at your core keep you anchored within and navigating along the eye of the storm rather than swirling among the damaging winds. I would count on a forecast of ever-increasing winds in the world ahead.

Specifics really do matter. They matter a whole lot.

[Should My Values Be Aspirational or Reflect My Current Conditions?]

Early on in the search for specifics, clarifying questions often surface from a place of guilt or dreaming. "Should my values be aspirational or reflect my current conditions?" is one of them. This question almost always comes from a place of good intent.

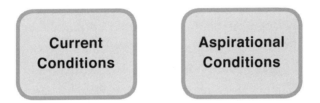

At the same time, it can also come from a place of disconnect. Especially if the question comes from a leader who has already sensed they have drifted. Which, of course, could apply to all of us.

It can also come from the misdirected wisdom contained in many a leadership book. In an attempt to cut to the chase of core values, these books suggest that if you want to know someone's core values, all you have to do is look at their checkbook or calendar; it's there that you'll see how they spend their money and their time. I've certainly fallen for this, and even suggested it to others.

It makes for a nice cliché. But it is a judgmental and damning proposition for others and ourselves.

We have no idea if someone's checkbook or calendar reflects the values at their core. We don't even know if our own checkbook and calendar reflect the values at our core. This is especially true if we have never taken a journey to our core. The reason has to do specifically with a concept we noted before: *the drift.*

Some leaders can put a wonderful spin on their checkbook and calendar to reflect an image or brand they wish to portray to others or to themselves. But that is far from the reality of their core.

We have no idea whether someone's checkbook, calendar, or both reflect unfettered drift or a set of values settled deep within. It might be either or a mixture of both. If their drift has gone on long enough or far enough, the drift and the corroded condition of their core may be well represented among those pages. But it's a dangerous and misguided mantra on which to judge others or ourselves.

It's a bad place to look and a horrible place to start.

So as you begin your journey, don't wonder if the values you are searching to find reflect aspiration or reflect your current condition. It's the wrong question and will send you down a path in the wrong direction.

You aren't searching for future aspirations or current conditions—you are actually searching for what is real. You are searching for what is true.

Once you find that truth, I have no doubt you will find the inspiration to move your current conditions (checkbook, calendar, and all) toward the truth of the values at your core.

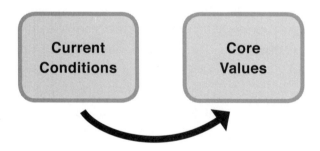

You won't find the truth overnight. Truth will find you over time. And you won't align your current conditions with your newly discovered values overnight. Those core values will help you align to them over time.

Your search will prove aspirational enough.

Getting Started: From "I Do" to "How To"

Leaders can effectively delegate specific items to trusted team members, or they can simply set out a directive for all to follow. Yet, leading the search for a Return On Integrity cannot be delegated or directed.

I love the title of Mac Anderson's book *Change Is Good . . . You Go First*. Every honest leader knows it rings a bell of personal truth. My friend and author Kevin Freiberg jests in putting it this way: *"Change is a good thing, as long as it's not happening to me!"*

> Be the change you wish to see in the world.

Let's just admit that it's a lot more fun to lead the change than to be the change. Perhaps that's why this quote by Mahatma Gandhi is one of the most repeated in the world: *Be the change you wish to see in the world.*

It's one of those quotes that never loses its commanding truth. It rings true for every human being, especially for leaders trying to build a Return On Integrity.

In our final section, *Destiny*, we will look at the "how to" in greater detail. It will give you a complete road map from beginning to forever (as there is no end) on how to build value with core values in such a way that you will clearly experience a real ROI. A Return On Integrity and, yes, a return on your investment.

Every executive fiber within you probably wants to jump to that section and get on with it. This is one jump you DO NOT want to make. I can guarantee it would be a quantum leap to a disastrous destiny.

When it comes to leading a Return On Integrity, *how to* can only begin with a leader's personal *I do*. There is no other way around it. If there were, we would see lots of examples where the leader at the top was able to just "inspire" everyone to connect to their core. From a leader's perspective, it would certainly feel more

> Leading the search for a Return On Integrity cannot be delegated or directed.

efficient, streamlined, and quickly scalable. It would get done, and once done, it would be finished. It could be checked off as another completed flavor of the month.

But we aren't talking about finishing something. We are talking about deeply living something. This takes time—*the leader's* time. *Your time* specifically. There are no effective detours. You have to genuinely experience it to effectively lead it. It won't always be pleasant, and at times it may be downright painful. There will be moments of confusion and guaranteed vulnerability. There will be doubts, followed by bursts of determination. You will be exposed. First to yourself by necessity, and then to everyone else by choice.

D———▷

Leaders start anyway.
═══════════

I propose this will be the most challenging leadership exercise you have privately and then publicly undertaken. Yet, there is no question that when your journey as a leader is complete, you will look back and see this personal experience as a turning point that defined the depth of the leadership legacy you leave behind.

When you look back, *and we all will,* you will understand that every second you invested provided a priceless return to you and everyone else. It just won't feel that way for a good while. Leaders start anyway.

Are you ready to commit to an "I DO" so you'll be fully prepared to lead others along a road map of "HOW TO"? If so, then let's do!

[A Blank Sheet of Paper]

Most people don't know their own core values. The same is true for most executives in positions of leadership. This is a fact I didn't anticipate. I always assumed intentional core values were in play. I think almost everyone makes this assumption. It's not the most dangerous assumption. The most dangerous assumption is that you actually know what your own core values are.

There is a really complicated and sophisticated assessment tool available to test your assumption. It's called—*a blank sheet of paper!*

If you want to evaluate whether someone knows their own personal core values, start with a simple question: "Do you think you know your own core values?" My experience is that most people will reactively reply with a tentative "I think so" or a confident "yes." If so, then just give them a blank sheet of paper and kindly say, "Name them." I have given this blank sheet of paper to thousands of people. My intention isn't to give that blank sheet of paper as a test; *it's to give it as a gift.* While most may feel like it's a test, they generally realize it's a wake-up call that exposes their own assumptions.

You will see what I mean when you first try to give it to your leadership team. You will see smart, analytical, successful, accomplished leaders start to stumble and grab for words. It's their silent alarm, their wake-up call, and your gift to them. It's not a gift they can return, because once unwrapped, the truth is out in the open. From that point forward their assumption is exposed.

Some will try to deny the truth, and some will try to make excuses. Others will pass it off as a cute team-building exercise. Others will chalk it up to their required annual submission to the development of their "soft" skills. Pay special attention to the ones who thank you.

You will understand all their various reactions because you will have personally experienced some of each of them from your own blank sheet of paper. How do I know that? Because I'm going to ask you now to get out a blank sheet of paper!

> **Pay special attention to the ones who thank you.**

It can be any sheet of paper, but I recommend one measuring 8½ by 11 inches. You might want to choose a nice sheet of paper, because this just may end up being a piece of paper you'll want to keep as a treasure for the remainder of your days as a leader and, hopefully, for the rest of your life. Not because it's a sheet where you completed the discovery of your core values, but rather the sheet where you started it.

To do this effectively, I want you to take the paper to a quiet area (if you are not already in one) and sit with it alone for thirty minutes. No phone, no tablet, no computer, and certainly no Google searches! Just you, your paper, and thirty completely uninterrupted minutes of your life.

In these thirty minutes, I want you to brainstorm any idea you think you might name as a value at your core. Write down any and every word that comes to mind. Do not filter, criticize, or prioritize any word you think of. Just write it down. I don't want you to worry whether a word is a behavior, want, need, or value. We'll get to that later. All I want you to do, now, is brainstorm with every fiber you can muster. At this stage, I want you to go for quantity, not quality. We'll also get to that later. I want you to try to keep your pen or pencil moving constantly for the whole thirty minutes.

Once you have completed this exercise, I want you to STOP reading this book—*for the next three days.* And during those next three days, I want you to find another ten minutes a day to review your brainstorm list and add any other words that might come to mind. That's another thirty minutes across these three days.

At the end of those three days, pick up where you left off and continue reading this book!

By the way, if you get stuck during that initial thirty-minute window of time or you draw a blank and your pen or pencil stops moving, just know that it's all part of the gift of the blank sheet of paper. Embrace it, own it, and know you are simply having a really bad case—*of normal!*

> **Now—stop reading, get your blank sheet of paper, and go start writing!**

Enjoy this incredibly valuable first and most important step on your way from "I DO" to "HOW TO" leadership.

Now—stop reading, get your blank sheet of paper, and go start writing!

[Exponentially Expanding Your Brainstorm]

There is no real leadership in the quest to building Return On Integrity if you ask others to do something that you haven't actually done yourself.

If it's not three days later, or you haven't completed the exercise described above, please finish reading this paragraph and then go back to the previous header, "A Blank Sheet of Paper," and reread it. Then finish the exercise over the next three days and come back and continue reading. I can't overemphasize how important this exercise is for you to move from "I DO" to "HOW TO" leadership in building your Return On Integrity. There is no integrity or real leadership in the quest to building Return On Integrity if you ask others to do something that you haven't actually done yourself. Leading a Return On Integrity comes from experience—your own personal experience. Any other approach diminishes your ability to lead this process. So, if you haven't completed the exercise, it's *crucial* that you stop (completely letting go of the fact that you tried to skip a really important step!) and just take your blank sheet of paper and begin again.

> There is no real leadership in the quest to building Return On Integrity if you ask others to do something that you haven't actually done yourself.

If it's at least three days later *and* you have completed the blank sheet of paper exercise . . . then let's keep going!

* * *

The experience you have just completed is the first, yet incredibly important, shovel scoop in starting to dig to your own personal core. It is also the first crucial step in escorting the collective organization you lead on a thousand-mile journey to the intersection of personal and organizational core values. It will be the first of many tests of your patience and persistence. Much like with a piece of fruit, you can't rush the ripening process.

This is one of those times. These ripening moments are not dormant seasons. Quite the opposite. They are active times of evolution, not times to rush to the next step in the process. The deeper you dig during the "I DO" segment of your journey, the more effective you will be at leading the "HOW TO" journey within your organization. Executives tend to want to quickly move on to execute the next item on their to-do list. My hope is that leaders are far more interested in impact than next steps. The next steps will happen in due time. It's important you are impacted by the personal dig for your own core values. This is not about a list. This is about time providing you opportunities for conversations, reflection, and further exploration.

I recommend you allot *no less than three months* for this part of the journey. I would prefer you take up to six months. You can tell I'm not kidding when I say it takes time! Don't worry, we'll get a lot done in those six months, but we need you to keep digging for your personal core values as we do other things. As I continue to explain and you continue to dig, I think you'll *see why*. I think you'll *know why* as you experience this stage of ripening. Once you've experienced this stage on a personal level, I know you will be more equipped to lead others on an organizational level.

So we continue . . . with more brainstorming. As I mentioned earlier, I have employed the simple blank sheet of paper experience with thousands of participants in hundreds of keynote presentations. Typically, because of time constraints, I give three minutes for their brainstorming. For the majority of participants, who are not grounded by the knowledge of their own core values, these three minutes give ample time for them to experience a significant wake-up call.

So we continue . . . with more brain-storming.

I then give them the opportunity to get up, move around, and gather in random groups of three to share the ideas on their lists. They then shift to different groups in quick ninety-second encounters. The vast majority affirm how hard the blank sheet of paper exercise was for them and confirm how their brainstorming accelerates exponentially when they start discussing it with others. They also admit that these are not conversations they regularly, or even periodically, experience in their personal or professional lives.

In the three-person discussion groups, participants have been able to add a number of new ideas to their brainstorming lists. I can't have all those participants here to meet you, but I wanted to be able to give you the collective insights from those gatherings. Over a period of two years, with audience permission, I compiled a cumulative list of the ideas they discovered in their own dig during the "blank sheet of paper" experience.

Much like your initial list, their combined list is a motley one composed of behaviors, needs, wants, and of course some core values. I have never edited the list. Whatever was turned in remains on the list (except for exact duplications), nor have I judged the contents of the list or prioritized the ideas. They are presented in alphabetical order to avoid doing so.

As a next step, I offer you this *Core Values Brainstorming List* online (http://BlumbergROI.com/tools) as a way to exponentially expand your own brainstorming of ideas, but more importantly to shake things up in your mind. I would recommend you stay in this ripening stage for a significant period of time—again, as little as three months, but possibly as much as six. There is no pressure to rush. Remember, time is on your side. You will eventually develop an internal barometer indicating how your personal big dig is progressing. Let's explore a possible approach for digging.

*   *   *

There is no single way to go about brainstorming. There are as many ways to do it as there are leaders starting to dig. However, here is a framework to get you started:

- **Print out the *Core Values Brainstorming List*.** It is helpful to be engaged with the list. Slowly read the words, letting

each sink in and help trigger your own words. Circle, under-
line, or highlight any words that resonate. On those sheets,
note whatever words of your own that come to mind. As you
think about each word, try to distinguish it as a behavior,
want, need, or core value. Mark each one as such. There is
no right or wrong answer, but an awareness or a pattern will
begin to emerge for you.

- **Start your Version 1.0 list.** After a thorough review of the
  list, it will be time to officially start your own Version 1.0 list.
  It is helpful to build your list by making entries under each of
  the following four categories: Core Values, Needs, Wants, and
  Behaviors. Some may want to set up these four columns in an
  electronic spreadsheet (e.g., Excel) so they can, with just a few
  keystrokes, easily move things about. Others prefer a real sheet
  of paper and a pencil and eraser. Either one works, and both
  will require a lot of trial, error, and adjustments. Pens don't
  seem to be that useful! We'll come back to how to distinguish
  among the four categories later. For now, just make a number
  of great gut guesses! Those will prove useful in the long run.

- **Connect with your list in several sessions.** This will be a long
  list, and time is on your side. As you continue digging, I would
  suggest small increments of time for this phase. The ideal
  increment would be a minimum of thirty minutes per sitting
  (to be sure you can immerse yourself in your thoughts), and no
  more than one hour, because focused thinking will wane after
  that. It would be ideal to engage in these sittings two or three
  times a week over the next month.

- **Find other times to let your mind wander.** Outside of your
  scheduled sittings, find other times when you can simply let
  your mind wonder about and wander through the possible
  values at your core. Throughout these early months, your mind
  will continually process ideas in the background. It is helpful

to periodically check in and bring them to the foreground. This could be while exercising, taking a shower, going for a run or walk, in prayer or meditation, with a glass of wine or mug of beer, or while flying from one destination to another. The point here is that you have plenty of opportunity to continuously stir your thinking so that different ideas can surface depending on varying types of days, moods, challenges, and accomplishments. It's all part of you chasing your core values until they eventually catch you!

[In Community with Other Leaders]

Solitude is a great place to enter into your core. Yet, others can be very helpful along the way too!

I'm going to play off an adapted version of a couple of credit card commercials—*Community has its benefits.* Connecting with other top leaders throughout your own dig will prove—*priceless.*

You probably connect with other top leaders all the time in business, social, and civic settings. But I'm referring to a different kind of connection. Something much deeper and much more vulnerable. I'm referring to a very small handful of other top leaders (outside of your organization) who are experiencing exactly the same process along with you.

Connecting helps on many levels: accountability, accessibility, and sustainability. I would recommend that you form a group of four, including yourself. Four is an ideal number for gathering a variety of viewpoints, and a size that allows no one to hide in the conversation.

Ideally, these might be leaders who are geographically nearby, since it will make connecting on a regular basis easier—maybe every other week or so. Or you could expand your geographical boundaries and select three other leaders who may live anywhere from coast to coast. Technology would allow you to meet virtually, but starting with an initial concentrated in-person gathering would always have more impact.

* * *

In writing the original manuscript for this book, I decided I would make a commitment to facilitate such a gathering four times a year. I believe there are three things that make for a powerful experience:

- **Location.** Hold your gathering in a remote location, free of distractions and the temptations to fill time with other activities (golf, tennis, boating, etc.). In fact, meeting in a very remote location that includes little other than nature is ideal. A significant portion of this book was written from a location where the closest grocery store (or almost anything else, for that matter) was thirty minutes away.

- **Schedule.** Create a schedule that allows for ample discussion time, along with plenty of time in solitude so that each participant has time to think through their own thoughts and to breathe in silence (more to come on this). See sample agendas at http://www.BlumbergROI.com/tools. Unlike other leadership gatherings, there is only ONE topic: *core values*. No other agenda items are allowed. I would recommend a minimum of three days together. There is something about being together two nights that makes a substantial difference; it's hard to explain, but it's true! Remember, time is your friend in all of this. There is nothing efficient about rushing any of this process. Only effectiveness matters. It is through time that effectiveness is created. It is also created through complete solitude and silence. Again, we'll get back to that later, but solitude and silence are vital to this particular segment of the process.

- **Confidentiality.** Gather a group of people who are willing to be deeply vulnerable under an agreement of airtight confidentiality. This confidentiality agreement binds in two ways. The obvious is the standard *What's said here, stays here.* The less obvious is that outside of this time together, you can't bring up a discussion someone has shared unless they bring it back up with you. This allows each individual to return to a very vulnerable discussion only if they specifically choose to do so.

*   *   *

From these three simple guidelines, you see why it is so important to choose your group very carefully so that you can experience the best return on your time together. At this point, I have two recommendations: that everyone in the group has not only read this book completely, but they have individually completed everything we have described up to this point. The thoughts, questions, and ideas they bring to the collective thinking are guaranteed to provide an exponential return!

What you will experience during this group time will define the experience you lead in your own organization. There may very well be a role each of you could play in helping one another unite voices across organizations. We'll get back to that later.

The sooner you plan your approach to capitalizing on the incredible benefits of doing this in a small community, the better. It will take a while to find the ideal combination of participants and then match the calendars of busy leaders. So get that started; and in the meantime, keep reading!

The Flow of Core Values

The direction of flow matters. The story of the Chicago River is a perfect example. In 1900, what seemed to be the impossible was accomplished. The flow of the river was reversed! It's possible the city of Chicago would not exist today had this not been done.

The Chicago River, like every river, was going to flow. In this case, the direction of the flow mattered. In those early years, the river held a significant amount of sewage and factory waste. When heavy rains caused the river to swell, the polluted waters flowed into Lake Michigan. This, in turn, polluted the source of drinking water for the surrounding communities. A tragic percentage of the population was killed from illnesses caused from the contaminated water supply.

This pollution happened time and time again. Everyone understood that the problem was not the actual source of the drinking water. That source was an incredible gift. The problem was the direction of the polluted flow of the Chicago River into that incredible source. Everyone knew the problem. It's just that the people believed reversing the flow was impossible.

Actually, that isn't totally true. Engineers and numerous "leaders" knew the flow could be reversed. What they also knew was that it would take an investment. They knew resources were going to be required in a time of community bankruptcies and a dearth of creativity and courage. So the river continued to flow, carrying the pollution that transformed a source of life into a source of death. For decades, thousands continued to die.

Flow happens. It's the direction of the flow that really matters.

That is, until 1900. In that year, the flow of the river was reversed. The problem was solved. While there continued to be polluted elements in the river, the contaminated water never made it into Lake Michigan. The drinking supply remained pure, and water began to flow from Lake Michigan into the Chicago River. Over the years, the reverse flow inspired a change in behaviors toward the introduction of pollution into the river itself. Flow happens. It's the direction of the flow that really matters.

We have a flow problem when it comes to core values! I have no doubt that true leaders fully understand this problem. They simply know that fixing it will take an investment. Yes, it does take some resources. Most importantly, it takes an investment of the leaders themselves.

* * *

Let's walk down to the banks of this river. It is a continuum that flows in one direction or the other. The direction of the flow is critical. In the illustration below, the source of the unhealthy flow is behavior driven. Along the way, the originally disciplined behaviors are polluted with ungrounded wants and needs, eventually flowing into a pool of unintentional core values.

Like Lake Michigan, our core values have the potential to provide a source for living when they are intentionally chosen. However, when left unintended, the flow begins with behaviors and eventually our core values become a polluted catchall.

After witnessing thousands of people naming their own core values through the blank sheet of paper assessment, it's clear to me there's not a lot of clear water at the ideal source. People simply don't have a lot of clarity when it comes to naming their specific core values. Do they believe they are values-based? Possibly. Do they have a gut feeling or an intuition? Maybe. Do they have details? Rarely.

At the other end of the river is a swirling logjam of behaviors. These behaviors are being driven by unfiltered pollutants made up of to-do lists, metrics, measurements, expectations in relationships, veneers to be polished, brands to be created, and messages to be spun. The momentum of pollutants that force the flow of behaviors across the waters of what could be honorable wants and needs is incredible. But soon those honorable wants and needs become polluted, corrupted, and eventually misguided in this flow.

In fact, these wants and needs become all intermingled in the turbulent flow of the rushing waters. In the rush of this unhealthy flow, we end up *needing what we want instead of wanting what we need.* That's what happens when flow is going in the wrong direction.

It's a problem when all of this mess is pouring into what was intended to be the source—our core values. Not instantly, but eventually, the values get polluted.

And what happens then? People die . . . inside.

All the while, leaders understand the problem. So does everyone else. Unfortunately, we've come to this place where no one believes the flow can be reversed.

Actually, that isn't totally true. I'm convinced leaders know it can be reversed. The problem is that we have a lot of followers in leadership positions and followers don't believe the flow can be reversed.

We need leaders that will step up to reverse the flow. And that is precisely the purpose of *Return On Integrity*: equipping leaders to reverse the flow.

Amazing things happen when we become clear about the specifics at the source of our core. From that core flows an essence that clarifies a healthy set of needs rightfully igniting fruitful wants and putting into action essential behaviors that are far more productive and effective.

The direction of flow matters. It's time to reverse the flow.

[Core Values, Needs, Wants, and Behaviors]

Once the flow is reversed, every element becomes less polluted and more important. One of the great challenges in creating your worksheet of values, needs, wants, and behaviors is diminishing the worth of anything outside of core values. It's important for us to understand that every one of these categories plays an important role.

When the flow is moving in the right direction, then the three categories outside of core values play an increasingly important and positive role. Each of them benefits by the direction set by the core. As you lay out your ideas, do not think that placing a word in a column other than core values makes that idea any less important. In effect, each of them becomes an expression of a value. They are connected and bring greater value when in sync with each other.

From my college days, I hold great memories of canoeing on the Spring River near Hardy, Arkansas. I'm not an expert at canoeing, but I do know that it's essential to know the flow of the river. If you want to end up at Point B, the flow tells you where your Point A drop-in location has to be.

When it comes to leadership development, we sometimes drop in at Point C, intending to get to B. If you have ever gone canoeing, you will know that going upstream is very difficult, tiring, and almost impossible. But in the spirit of short-term efficiencies, we unintentionally undermine long-term effectiveness.

All the points along the river are important, but it's critical to know which is which.

Let me share a simple example just to illustrate. Let's assume no one in the room at team meetings thinks Joe listens. Everyone wants Joe to become a better listener. So we ship Joe off to a class on improving listening skills. It seems like a logical solution on the surface (of the water). But the real problem is that Joe has reverse flow.

> All the points along the river are important, but it's critical to know which is which.

So, the mechanics of "effective" listening are poured into Joe. He's working hard at listening to everything the instructor is telling him. He is rowing upstream through every module, but keeping his pace. Flexing his muscles, he demonstrates his mastery of each technique through role-play after role-play.

The instructor is impressed with her star pupil. Joe is pretty pleased with himself. He can't wait to not only get back to work but get home to demonstrate his newfound tools of manipulation. Joe is fascinated with his new ability to get people to think he is actually listening. He had no idea how beneficial this was going to be—and how naive he really thinks his teammates can be.

Joe may very well have a listening problem. But the bigger issue is a flow problem. And no matter how much we try to flood Joe with forced new behaviors, he will never arrive where we need him to be—or where he needs himself to be!

Instead of just dropping Joe in at the closest point, let's say we are going to invest in a van ride to take him well upstream to Point A. Joe is not going to like it. He is going to put up a fight and convince himself that on such a hot day he'll get carsick in that big van. You give him a barf bag and tell him to get in anyway. Against what he perceives as his better judgment, he gets in.

Amazingly, Joe doesn't get sick at all. He just sits in the van, rides along, mindlessly trying to ignore his negative thoughts. Bored at staring at the back of the seat in front of him, he glances out the window. Slowly he starts to notice some impressive expressions of nature. He sees some things he hasn't noticed in many years. There are unique and colorful flowers, trees soaring to the sky, a group of deer, and a family laughing and sharing a picnic together. They almost look unfamiliar. Joe realizes he has seen all of this before, but from his viewpoint in the polluted waters, he doesn't recognize any of it.

He spends the rest of the van ride thinking about bygone years along with those friends and family who made those years so memorable. He thinks of outings and vacations where he enjoyed sitting around and listening to jokes and stories he's heard a thousand times. He remembers how he walked along the beach during spring break with his best friend, and how they talked for hours into the night about hopes and dreams and fears. Back then he listened and learned and loved every minute of it.

Joe is deep in thought when he realizes his name is being called—louder and louder with each call. *Joe, get out! We've arrived at Point A.* He feels a twinge of guilt at being caught not listening again. He steps out of his train of thought and then out of the van.

He walks over to the water and begins to stare at the water rushing from the river's source. The water gives off a sense of energy that inspires Joe and opens his being, his very core. He looks deeper into the reflections the sun's bright rays have brought forth.

There are no instructors, no other participants, no well-timed, neatly crafted role-plays designed to practice a new skill. Joe is alone with the flowing river and the feeling that he doesn't need to learn something new, but needs to rediscover something he once had before. He moves closer to the edge of the river, where the water is rushing. He takes off his shoes, rolls up his pants legs, and sits down on a rock. The water sprays against his legs in a playful and inviting way. It feels refreshing. It has been a very long time since Joe sat on the bank at the source of a river. Come to think of it, Joe couldn't really remember the last time he's sat down alone or with someone else at the source of anything really meaningful.

He stands up and steps into the water. While looking downstream, Joe feels a huge rush of water from upstream slam against his back. He's soaked and almost knocked flat-faced into the river. As he grabs a large rock to catch his balance, he feels a sense of something in his soul he hasn't felt in a while—respect. The need to respect the river.

He gets to his feet, stops, and thinks about the idea of respect; he recalls endless examples of how respecting other people has brought great joy to his life. He thinks of the diverse nature of his friends and how much he's drawn from those relationships. He's always been seen as someone who respects all those he meets. Teachers, coaches, friends, classmates, and family alike have taken great strength from Joe's natural inclination to respect everyone. As he stands there in the river, he reconnects to his experience of respecting others and is reminded that respect is a value rooted deep within his core.

But over time, the unchecked demands of Joe's life have reversed his flow. This flood of demands has stirred up messy particles of unfounded needs, misguided wants, and frivolous desires, resulting in an array of bad behaviors.

After seeing this, Joe walks back over the bank and sits down again at the edge of the river—at the source. He watches the direction the water was flowing and realizes he doesn't need to be better at the skill of listening; he simply needs to reconnect to the respect he knew so well within his core. When he reconnects to that core, that respect, he has no doubt he will know exactly how to listen. He realizes that while listening is a skill, it is more importantly a reflection of a core value—one he's been neglecting.

And that value, respect, is the source of a range of other effective behaviors that can flow out wherever and whenever he calls upon them.

Likewise, leaders of organizations can waste enormous resources when we don't understand this issue of flow. We try to cure the perceived problem by pouring more skill sets into the polluted waters flowing in an unhealthy direction. We push off on others the hard task of identifying the problem, under a pretense of delegation because we don't have the courage to personally invite them on a journey up to Point A to investigate where the good water flows from the river's source.

It's not only a waste. It's a shame and a failure of leadership.

Behaviors, wants, and needs become diminished and polluted when they don't flow from the source of core values. However, when they do, they can become far more valuable than any teachable skill. When we understand that skills are expressions of our core and not manipulations of other people, we begin to build a Return On Integrity. It is nearly impossible to lead a follower to Point A if you have never been there yourself.

A riverbank is a great place for you to sit and rest. You might be surprised, as you sit there searching, what may find you. In doing so, you may begin to see the richness in each and every category—behaviors, wants, needs, and the core values from which they all should flow.

[Fine-Tuned Distinctions]

Let's go back to your four columns titled Core Values, Needs, Wants, and Behaviors. They are not isolated silos. They are not black-and-white buckets. And ultimately, there are not right or wrong answers as to what words fall into which buckets.

Each of the buckets is important. It is common for someone to ask, "How many core values am I supposed to have?" My first response is, "No more than you can remember!" It is hard to live a value you can't remember. It seems many people end up with somewhere between three and seven core values. There is no right answer to the question of how many, but they must be in a memorable quantity. Often, we lump too many words into the core-values bucket because we consider the other three columns of less importance. In their own right, all of the buckets are important.

It seems most people want black-and-white answers to fill these columns. If it were that easy, it would actually prove to be less helpful. The exercise of the four columns is designed to create an awareness of your own personal *Destiny Road Map*. This is where an electronic spreadsheet (e.g., Excel) or a piece of paper with a sharp pencil and a big eraser may prove helpful. You will begin to see connections between certain values and the needs, wants, and behaviors that may flow from them. You may experience a clear connection just as Joe did in our short example of seeing how listening was a behavior that flowed from respect. Sometimes it may not be that clear. Think of your worksheet as a jigsaw puzzle—you have to experiment by trying out the pieces in different places. It's all part of the discovery as you keep digging to your core.

Some find the notion of asking "Why?" to be very helpful. Not judgmental why questions that others might ask of you, but the inquisitive why questions you ask of yourself.

In the 1990s there was a management theory called TQM. It meant Total Quality Management. TQM involved a lot of intentional measurements that, no doubt, put a lot of unintentional pressure on personal and organizational core values that had probably rarely been thought about.

It's important to note here that if the river is flowing in the wrong direction, it doesn't matter how much you measure the water. Often, measuring will do more harm than good.

Tucked within the philosophy of TQM, however, was this little theory of *why*. It was brilliant!

You might actually think of it as a more complicated formula of why^5. But then again, it wasn't that sophisticated. It was pretty simple and very useful. It simply stated that if there is a problem in an organization, you have to ask the "why" question five times to get to the real problem.

So let's say something goes wrong. You would ask . . . so *why* did that happen? Then with the answer to that question, you would ask . . . so *why* did that happen? Then with the answer to that second question, you would ask *why* again . . . and again . . . and for a fifth time ask it again. The theory was that the answer to that fifth *why* (or why^5) was the real problem and everything else was just a symptom of that problem. The idea purported that until you fixed the why^5 problem, you would continue to experience all the other symptoms. It's useful to note here, as in our example with Joe, that we often work on the symptoms of behaviors rather than digging to the core issue.

Yet, it might be helpful to take the concept of "why" and apply it to a whole new context of your four columns of Core Values, Needs, Wants, and Behaviors. Try to create a systematic flow on your worksheet that makes some sense to you.

Take a word on your brainstorm list . . . any word. Ask yourself *why* this is really important to you. If there is an answer, you have likely moved one step closer from the behavior side of your puzzle toward the core-value side of the puzzle. Then take that answer and ask the question *Why is this word so important to me?* If there is an answer, again you have likely moved one step closer from the behavior side of your puzzle toward the core-value side. I don't know if you will actually make it through five *whys*. But I do know that at some point you will ask the *why* question and there will be no answer. You will ponder and finally say . . . there is no answer . . . *it just is.* At that point, you are most likely at the level of a very deep need or a core value. This process is simply one way to test out the pieces of your puzzle.

Sometimes, asking *why* is part of the hard digging needed to reverse the river's flow.

You will likely find that working with your four-column worksheet is not a one-way linear process. It is helpful to work at it from all sides . . . trying it from all directions.

For instance, some like to try it from the other direction. Take a word that seems to be speaking to you as a core value. Let's take that word and work the other direction. Here, we can discover what flows from it. Let's go back to Joe's rediscovery of respect at his core. Here (instead of *why*), we substitute the word "because." Follow this flow:

Respect is core *because* I need connection.
Connection is a need *because* I want to engage.
Engage is a want, and *therefore* I will be a great listener.

While helpful in navigating the flow of your puzzle, this "because" approach can actually send you drifting if you are not careful, especially if you don't keep it "others-focused." In the example above, the focus still remains on others. If it becomes "about you," then what you find is that even a slight drift introduces pollutants into the mix that can easily begin to use your values in a manipulative way for personal gain. Checking the nature and purity of your motives helps keep the pollutants out of the flow.

You may find it helpful to assign a brief description to each of the column headings so you can keep them differentiated in your mind. Examples might include the following:

- A behavior is *action-oriented* and is put into motion in specific situations. You might think of its application as being very situational.

- A want is a *desire* for something, someone, or somewhere.

- A need is very *foundational* in nature and is embedded so deeply that it may feel like a value. You can often see a very direct connection to a value. If not twins, they are first cousins.

- A value tends to be a very personal principle that when consistently applied sets a *trajectory* into motion. A flow, you might say! It is what establishes integrity, because integrity is the fabric of each and every value.

Once established, embraced with commitment and a grasp of personal ownership, each value is like a dye poured into the flowing water of the river. It penetrates everything—every need, every want, and every behavior.

This integration is critical. You will find that almost any need, want, or behavior that is not grounded to your core values can easily become polluted and slowly, but surely, once again will start to reverse the flow. That's precisely how the drift begins.

It might help to start with these basic parameters. Again, it's important that you don't think of the columns on your worksheet as black-and-white buckets. As you work with your list, you will find themes, then insights, and then wisdom begin to surface. It might be helpful for us to go back to our symbol of looking at a prism from many sides, or into the lens of a kaleidoscope. That is why several periodic sittings with your list will give you fresh perspectives, allowing you to reflect from several different angles. When you are trying to reverse the flow, you can see that it's important to keep the discovery process itself fluid.

It can get frustrating and confusing at times. It's the fluidity of the process that changes the flow. I'm sure it wasn't easy reversing the flow of the Chicago River. But it saved many lives and laid the foundation of a great city.

[The Interrelational Nature of Core Values]

While we may come to the insight of our core values one at a time, they will ultimately become a package deal. They work in unison with one another. While core values bring strength to your needs, wants, and behaviors, they bring the most strength to each other when they are integrated.

This means your core values influence one another from the very source of the river. It is helpful to consciously think about how each of your core values influences all the other core values on your list. You will find opportunities to bring further depth to your values by doing this. It is this intentional integration that makes your core uniquely you!

At the same time, you will find contradictions. At least, that is how they appear on the surface. And if not contradictions, you will feel like one value may compete with another. And it will certainly feel that way in certain situations as you are trying to live them.

For the sake of clarity, I like to think of them as combined resources. In any given situation, one value may need to take the lead, while never being disconnected from any of the others. Any value taking the lead is still accountable to all the other values with which it is integrated. It's important that your own core values remain integrated too.

But that doesn't mean that in any given situation they are in perfect balance.

I remember a conversation years ago with my friend Kevin. We were talking about the big trend at that time, which was to create "balance in your life." Kevin's perspective always stuck with me. He said, "I believe this 'balance thing' is a figment of our imagination. Life is more like a pendulum that swings back and forth. It isn't about balance, it's about keeping your eye on the pendulum and asking if it is where it should be at the time."

I didn't realize it then, but doing as he said would be hard, if not impossible, if you weren't clear on your own core values. I would say the strength of your core values is the best diagnostic tool of your pendulum. Sometimes one value takes the lead while still remaining accountable to all the others. It's the only way they remain integrated—it's precisely why integrity is not a core value. Rather, *it is the fabric of every value.*

It doesn't happen automatically. It must happen intentionally every day.

[3-D Values Activation]

It's easy to make this entire process an exercise you embrace completely— *and then put away.* You would think that once you dive so deeply to establish a set of values and reverse the flow of the river, things would just—flow. If only it were so easy.

A dear friend, Dr. Tom Nelson, is a family medical doctor. As part of his medical practice, he has introduced a process called "Self Activation Technique," or SAT (www.activateanddominate.com). The theory is that diaphragmatic breathing and certain pressure points can create an inside-out integrity in our neuromuscular system. Dr. Tom would describe the muscle activation process as one that allows the "physical core" of our bodies to do all the hard work. Otherwise, the flow gets compromised and the body starts demanding that other parts of itself take on heavy loads they were never meant or designed to carry. What separates SAT from other types of muscle activation is the ongoing work that can and must be done on your own in order to remain in proper muscle sequence flowing from your physical core.

This makes for a perfect analogy when it comes to our core values.

Our values have to be activated on a regular basis. Otherwise, the flow gets messed up again. Instead of our core values doing the driving, the burden shifts to our needs, wants, and behaviors. And just like the non-core parts of our body, they will try to pick up a load they were never designed to carry. But they certainly will pick them up anyway—and have a heavy price to pay later.

We'll get back to the "how" of this values activation later.

*   *   *

Digging for your personal core values is like digging a 100-foot-deep water well. The first thing you need to realize is that the water is there *whether you choose to dig for it or not.* It is always an intentional choice. But digging is really hard work. It can get very discouraging along the way. You dig 5 feet and you are still looking at dirt. But with your determination you keep digging. You get to 35 feet and you are still looking at dirt. You will feel discouraged, but your leadership mindset tells you to keep digging. At 75 feet you are still looking at dirt. Now you're miffed, feeling this whole thing is pointless and has left things more confusing and discouraging than ever. You are in a deep hole by now and decide you might as well keep digging. Then . . . at 100 feet you see water. It is there that you tap into the fuel for your leadership.

> **The first thing you need to realize is that the water is there *whether you choose to dig for it or not.***

Defining your core values is a crucial moment in your life. It's actually a period of time that intentionally reverses the flow. It redefines the source. It's part of the beginning. Remember that "flow" is a constant process. It will take an everyday commitment to keep the flow moving in the right direction. We'll get to that everyday commitment later. For now, just remember that the direction and quality of the flow are determined by defining the source.

5

Realizing Why Personal Values Aren't Just Personal

If you want to understand how "non-personal" personal values can
be, just ask someone who has been part of an organization where
there has been a breakdown at the core. The majority will tell you
that the "personal values" of a few systemically impacted everyone.
That, in and of itself, becomes very personal for everyone impacted!

A t some point, the executive side of us is bound to kick in and question what all this personal stuff has to do with organizations and our work. In fact, after covering so much ground on the very personal front (without a mention of the organization), I'm surprised you're still reading this book! It must be the leader inside of you! I'm sure some executives have cast it aside by now. After all, who would blame them, with all the organizational pressures bearing down upon executives in today's world? There's a part of me that fully understands how this very natural temptation would be so easy to succumb to.

It had to seem overwhelming to think of reversing the flow of the Chicago River. It must have seemed a lot simpler, to those charged with the daunting task, just to find a way to disassociate the sick and dying from the water.

Surely there had to be lots of other reasons people were getting sick. After all, people get sick. That's just the way it is. Forget the flow of the river, and let's work on getting some more meds and beds for all these dying people!

But a true leader would relentlessly acknowledge the connection, and keep a clear vision and an efficient strategy for reversing the flow. The leader's core would continue to flow against a rising tide of weak conventional wisdom.

The meds and beds solution is not a whole lot different from simply plugging in a few more training programs to ramp up more skills, to mechanically rally alignment, to infuse engagement, and to execute a service mind-set.

Even so, this leader may still question why we have remained focused on the personal side of this equation for so long. Somewhere along the way, it may dawn on her to think, *Aren't personal values . . . um, personal?* Yes, they are. But don't forget, they are also systemic, whether you want them to be or not.

Establishing a Valuable Connection

Organizational core values alone are never enough. Even organizations with long-established organizational values have failed to understand the risk in ignoring the powerful impact of personal values. Personal core values are never left at the entrance of any organization, however hard you may wish to ignore them.

No matter how much we try to establish proper directional flow with organizational core values, if personal core values are ignored, there will always be the risk of an unhealthy undertow shifting the flow of everything. None of this will be intentional, but all of it will be real.

Over time, the undertow will begin to strengthen on its own, and before long the intentional flow of organizational values will lose strength, become irrelevant, and finally change direction. And when the flow is moving in the wrong direction, the pollution goes in all directions. Unfortunately, the pollution is often not discernable until it's too late.

And because core values are so personal, it's precisely what makes their systemic organizational nature either completely lethal . . . *or packed full of enormous potential!*

> If you were to take only one idea away from this book, I hope it would be this: The reason most organizational core values have provided limited value is because the personal part of the equation has been ignored or cast aside as not relevant.

If you were to take only one idea away from this book, I hope it would be this: The reason most organizational core values have provided limited value is because the personal part of the equation has been ignored or cast aside as not relevant.

The bottom-line truth when it comes to core values is, there's really no such thing as an organization—period. An organization is, ultimately, nothing more than a collection of people. That gets very personal, whether we like it or not. There's no question, over time, that an organization takes on a personality we call culture, but let's be clear—it remains a collection of people.

Does this mean that organizational values are meaningless? Not at all. They are a call to the collective way of getting things done. They are the fuel for defining the organization's culture. The organization's core values will, however, always be less effective if they are not fueled by the known personal values of each and every individual in the organization.

The personal core values of the leader and each person on the team will eventually determine the fabric of the official organizational core values. It is critical for a leader to understand and then lead this systemic connection between personal and organizational core values.

Over time, the direction of the flow will either make people worse or make them better. A leader who intentionally takes ownership for the direction of the flow determines the difference.

[The Organizational Impact of Personal Values]

Both personal and organizational core values are in motion. This is true regardless of the direction of the flow of values, needs, wants, and behaviors we previously discussed. Attention to neither, or to one without the other, impacts their powerful influence on this flow. It will be unintentionally driven by *reaction* or intentionally driven by *response*. Let's explore this subtle yet impactful nuance.

There are two predicable scenarios leaders can count on as they begin this process:

- Most people won't know their own personal core values. Are they values-based? Likely. Do they have a gut feeling or intuition? Possibly. Do they have a grasp of the specifics? Probably not.

- Most people would much rather discuss organizational core values than think about their own personal core values.

The first scenario has a lot to do with the reason for the second. I have come to realize there is another very human factor at play here.

When it comes to solely having organizational core values—we *react* to them. They're still outside us. We can hold them up and look at them, cognitively judge them, and, most conveniently, judge others with them. People often wait and see if others, especially "the executive team," live these organizational values. If they do, then maybe they'll think about living them too. Unfortunately, few give the organizational core values much thought at all.

There is a good reason for this common trap. Very few have ever experienced a leader who engages personal and organizational core values as their most strategic and impactful resource. For most, there just isn't a prior experience they can draw from. They have simply never seen the river reverse directions. It's not even a matter of deciding if the reverse flow would be possible—most have never thoughtfully sat on the river-bank to even notice there was a flow in play at all.

It isn't just that personal values have not been made part of the equa-tion. While it's true most people don't know the specifics of their per-sonal core values or have ever been challenged to discover and put them into organizational play, most couldn't tell you the specific values of their organization either.

To make matters worse, the same could be said for most executive teams. They would be in the same boat, floating along in who-knows-what direction!

There's a very cost-effective way to test this premise. Remember? *It's called a blank sheet of paper!*

If the organization's core values are known, they are often put forth and used as an inconsistent method of enforcement or compliance. In that sense, organizational core values can make for strong tools—even weapons—*of judgment.* It's sure easier (and a lot more fun!) when, as with gossip, we can use organizational core values as a measurement stick *against others.* And when intentional personal core values are not in play, it's a lot more likely that this will happen.

For other organizations, that may not be their experience at all. They fall into the trap of making values the exception by honoring "the living of them" in grand ways! They may have wonderful awards of recognition at quarterly meetings for employees who have displayed an example of a behavior that demonstrates an organizational value. That, in itself, ought to be our biggest red flag—that living organizational core values is such a unique event that it deserves an award when it actually happens!

The absence of a personal connection to organizational core values makes it an "exceptional" practice. There is a reason for this. Because organizational core values are "outside of us," we will naturally *react* to them. Reactions tend to be situational rather than transformational. Ethics training and case studies only reinforce a situational application of values being a description of "what" we do rather than "who" we are. While it's a good practice to invest in an insurance policy, it furthers a situational and reactionary mind-set. Often the discussions and conclusions of such exercises draw on gut reactions rather than intentional connections to a list of organizational core values that most can't remember.

Personal core values are different. When we do the hard work of digging for them, discerning them, investigating them, test-driving them, claiming them, and finally owning them, we *respond* to them. They are "inside us." We have discovered them, we have come to know them, we have embraced them, and now we own them. The natural flow of who we are becomes a *response*, rather than a situational *reaction*. This alone changes everything.

[The Personal to Organizational Flow]

The hardest part of this process for a leader is staying engaged in the exercise of discerning, investigating, and beginning to test-drive personal core values before shifting to organizational core values.

It takes patience and persistence to do this. Yet, there is a very valid reason why this is so important. It's that flow thing again.

I have often seen executives actually gravitate to a written copy of their organization's core values in an attempt to try to discover their own personal core values. They, of course, will look for a written copy, since a recall by memory fails most! While not necessarily written on their heart and soul, they will usually claim a sense of familiarity with the organization's core values when they see them in the written form. They will note their gut feeling or natural intuition about those values.

Most executives usually have some sense of responsibility about having a familiar connection to the values. And thus, when asked to think about their personal values, they often use these organizational values as a reference point.

On the surface, this might seem like a safe resource. However, when your self-identity comes from the outside, rather than the inside, your flow is headed in the wrong direction. We'll see later that organizational core values serve as a positive reinforcement to personal core values, but should never be the *source* of your personal core.

This is precisely why *personal* core values are the place where we begin. It's not that the flow from personal core values determines an organization's core values, but they are the fuel that enables organizational core values to be genuinely lived each and every day. There is a natural flow to our own personal continuum—from values to needs to wants and then behaviors. Likewise, there is a natural flow from personal to organizational core values.

This is the reason it must start with the leader and the leader must start with personal core values before anything else.

[A Collectively Valuable Trajectory]

The flow we'll describe here naturally congregates in a pool of trust. There's been plenty written on the topic of trust, and these writings rightfully declare the solid business reasons behind the value of trust.

Like values, trust is a prism with many facets. Some believe trust must be earned. Others believe it's honorable to give it away. From a leadership perspective, both angles of this trust prism have their place. I would suggest the values in our personal core determine the angle from which we view the prism.

I would also suggest that while trust is incredibly valuable, *it's not a core value*. It's a critical need fueled by the intentional and continual flow of personal and organizational core values.

When the organizational river is flowing in the right direction, it looks like this:

It begins with the challenging, yet refreshing, work of identifying our *personal core values*. Once we have genuinely connected with our personal core values and understand the authentic value they can bring, it's natural for us to be drawn with interest into the *core values of others*. Not to judge them, but to know them and understand them.

It is genuine interest, such as this, that builds meaningful connections, genuine collaboration, and shines a light on the deeper common ground of a diverse and multi-generational workforce. It is the ultimate team-building exercise where no outdoor adventure is needed, although such an adventure would be meaningfully enhanced if personal and organizational core values went along for the ride!

It's with this understanding of our personal core values, and a connection to the core values of others, that we begin to see *organizational core values* through a completely different lens. I have challenged thousands to do the hard work on discovering their own personal core values *and then* to look at the stated core values of their organization through the lens of their personal core values.

I then asked them to test my premise. I suggest that by looking through the clear lens of their personal core values, they will see the organizational values in a richer way than they have ever seen them before.

They will find, through this lens, the insight to personally own the organizational core values. It is at this intentional intersection that we take the organizational core values, created on the outside, and bring them to our inside. It is here we begin to *respond* to personal *and* organizational core values alike, and no longer merely react to either.

It is at this intersection (this connection) that an organization provides the opportunity for employees to know, understand, own, and hold themselves and then others accountable to the organizational core values. This is the intersection where natural alignment is seeded and the reality of integrity is fueled. It's the integration of the two sets of core values that sparks authentic engagement.

When everyone engages in this process, we see the concept of *shared values* begin to emerge and be understood. This is not a set of values diluted in the mix of all the values pooled together. It is, rather, a strong current flowing in the right direction, fully engulfing the diversity of strong personal values and bringing to life the organizational values in lots of unique ways. Each individual engages, through the lens of their own personal core values, in how they uniquely can bring each organizational core value to life every day.

In this process of discovery, a few may find there is no intersection at all. In that case, they may very well have discovered they are in the wrong place. It's their responsibility to either find the intersection or find a different environment that does intersect with their personal core values. When there is no intersection and no one acts on it, everyone loses.

For the majority who discover the intersection of their personal and organizational core values, trust naturally surfaces into the mix of this flowing current.

But none of this happens unless we first do the hard work, upstream, of digging for and identifying our personal core values. It's hard to know others when you don't know yourself. It's easier to trust others when they know themselves and you know who they know themselves to be.

This entire trajectory starts first with one person: the leader. Then the leader does what leaders do: Lead others to do the same.

Organizational Core Values

Many organizations name an official set of core values. It can be the sign of a great commitment, the reality of a big assumption, or a facade of what they want others to believe. I may be naive, but I believe this facade is rare. While incredibly unhealthy, in some ways it has its advantages because it's intentional and its motives are clear. While it may fool some on the outside for a period of time, it doesn't have the same potential for deceit on the inside. While the official values may not be real, the motives behind them reveal a set of unstated core values that are unfortunately understood completely within the organization.

Real leaders understand that core values are the business.

More frequently, we find the vast majority of organizations publicly naming a set of core values; but that's it—*they just name them.* The reality is that many executive teams feel they have honored their responsibility by simply *establishing* the core values. Just getting them out there! And then they get back to business. Real leaders understand that core values are the business.

There is no place to go back to—you never left the business to create the values—the business lives and thrives in the midst of the values. It's imperative to embrace this reality as you are establishing the organization's core values.

Like personal core values, organizational core values are not a nice team-building exercise or an executive feel-good activity for an expensive getaway retreat. Organizational core values are not a branding exercise for the marketing department, or an assignment for the "softer side of things" initiated or executed by the human resources department.

Organizational core values are the sole responsibility of the leader—the CEO in publicly or privately held companies, the owner in an entrepreneurial adventure, or the leader at the very top of any organization. It's not another item on the to-do list. It's a powerful strategy waiting to be used—the most untapped and impactful strategy within the reach of any real leader.

This is precisely the reason the leader's experience in establishing his or her personal core values must precede addressing the organizational core values. A leader who hasn't established her own personal core values (and, just as importantly, hasn't lived the authentic struggle of doing so) is in no position to lead the development of the organization's core values, much less live them out each day and lead others to do the same.

> **Not now or ever will there be a time to delegate this process to a "well-prepared team," or any team, for that matter.**

It is my recommendation that a leader also lead her team of direct reports through the process of establishing their own personal values before ever engaging them in a discussion of organizational core values. It's only from there that a leader and her team are in a position to genuinely begin an authentic discussion of organizational core values.

Remember, this journey takes patience and persistence—but it is well worth it!

It's from here that a *leader* is prepared to engage with his team to *lead* and facilitate the process for the broader organization. Not now or ever will there be a time to delegate this process to a "well-prepared team," or any team, for that matter.

> **There is only one keeper of the soul—of the core—of the organization: the leader.**

The leader owns the process from the very beginning (including his own personal beginning) and should never delegate or relegate the process. And just like the ownership of the process, the process itself never, *ever* ends.

I used to think the CEO was the keeper of the organization's vision and the human resources department was the keeper of the soul. *I was completely wrong.*

There is only one keeper of the soul—of the core—of the organization:

the *leader*. Any other scenario undermines and eventually diminishes the value of organizational core values.

[Creating an Intentional Process]

Creating organizational core values is not an initiative. It is not a branding exercise. It is not a goal to be reached. I would recommend that you carefully and intentionally avoid each of these terms and anything like them in the language you use.

Defining core values simply sets in motion an intentional way of living both personally and in the business of the organization. And to do so requires an intentional process. I will define an overarching process to consider in the next section, *Destiny*. In the meantime, I do think there are some cornerstones to consider in preparing for that process.

[Establishing Current Condition]

When it comes to core values, every organization has a current condition. Every organization has a set of core values, whether they are intentionally stated or established by an inevitable, unhealthy reverse flow. The first step on the organizational side of the equation is assessing, with brutal honesty, the current condition.

Let's start our assessment by answering the following twenty-one questions. Note the "if so" nature of these questions. I would suggest there is a sequential nature to this assessment. At whatever point you reach your first "no" answer, you can pause to note that you have established your current condition. You might find answering the remaining questions interesting and informative, but it will not really be relevant to your analysis of the current condition. Those remaining questions will prove critically helpful in establishing a specific threshold to head toward. It won't be reached as a goal; it will be reached because you intentionally chose to lead the reversal of the flow. Take a few minutes to thoughtfully answer each question.

* * *

1. Do we currently have a stated set of core values?

2. If so, could I, as the leader, list each value on a blank sheet of paper?

3. If so, are these values fully known and understood by me?

4. If so, do I consciously and intentionally live each of the stated, known, and understood organizational core values, and am I painfully aware of it when I don't?

5. If so, could each member of my leadership team list each value on a blank sheet of paper?

6. If so, are these values fully known and understood by each member of my leadership team?

7. If so, does each member of my leadership team consciously and intentionally live each of the stated, known, and understood organizational core values, and are they painfully aware of it when they don't?

8. If so, could 98 percent of our employees list each value on a blank sheet of paper?

9. If so, are these values fully known and understood by 98 percent of our employees?

10. If so, do 98 percent of our employees consciously and intentionally live each of the stated, known, and understood organizational core values, and are they painfully aware of it when they don't?

11. If so, could my leadership team strongly agree that I live our set of stated, known, and understood organizational core values?

12. If so, could 98 percent of our employees strongly agree that I live our set of stated, known, and understood core values?

13. If so, could 98 percent of our employees strongly agree that each member of my leadership team lives our set of stated, known, and understood core values?

14. If so, do I, as the leader, believe our organizational core values build value?

15. If so, does each member of my leadership team believe that our organizational core values build value?

16. If so, would 98 percent of our employees believe that our organizational core values build value?

17. If so, do I, as the leader, consciously think about our organizational core values when I make everyday choices, strategic decisions, and show up in internal and external relationships?

18. If so, does each member of my leadership team consciously think about our organizational core values when they make everyday choices, strategic decisions, and show up in internal and external relationships?

19. If so, do 98 percent of our employees consciously think about our organizational core values when they make everyday choices, strategic decisions, and show up in internal and external relationships?

20. If so, is the specific language of our organizational core values verbally used on a regular basis and as a reference point and guiding light?

21. If so, are the language, spirit, and essence of each of our stated

organizational core values relevant, engaging, inspiring, and reflective of a robust core?

Think long and hard on this last question. The first twenty questions are a quantitative assessment of the commitment to the values—however they are stated. This last question (question twenty-one) is a qualitative assessment of the effectiveness in how the core values are stated.

Without the commitment, the qualitative nature of the values is not much use. However, without a rich qualitative component, a strong commitment may not be achieving anywhere close to its full potential.

Regardless of your answer to question twenty-one, it would serve you well to completely reevaluate an existing list of stated organizational core values. You might think of it as each currently stated value having to earn its way back onto a clean slate. If there are no stated organizational core values, it's the perfect time to build one from scratch.

There are three final questions critical to assessing the current condition of the intersection of personal and organizational core values. Affirmative answers to these questions aren't possible if there isn't a stated set of organizational core values to begin with. A negative answer to question twenty-one, of course, would have a qualitative impact on any affirmative responses to the first twenty questions, but also on any affirmative responses to these three questions.

You will find embedded within that twenty-first question the very recipe for helping each of the final three questions meet their full potential.

22. Do I have, know, fully understand, and live a set of personal core values intentionally intersected into our organizational core values?

23. Does each member of my leadership team see themselves as knowing, fully understanding, and living a set of personal core values intentionally intersected into our organizational core values?

24. Do 98 percent of our employees see themselves as knowing, fully
understanding, and living a set of personal core values intentionally intersected into our organizational core values?

We previously said that holding up your values and looking at them
is like holding up a prism while turning it to see a variety of perspectives.
Having an affirmative answer to all twenty-four questions is like turning
your prism into a diamond—a 24-carat diamond!

[Establishing a Core Team]

While it's important for the leader to personally lead this effort, it can be
very beneficial to engage others. We will later talk about establishing an
Organizational Core Values Team. So, who should be tapped in the process of evaluating and/or establishing a set of organizational core values?

This will depend on a number of variables, with one exception. The
choice needs to be both strategic and intentional. There will be parameters
that need to be considered in various types of organizations. In all cases,
it's a matter of considering which specific people should be involved. In
some cases, it's a matter of bylaws or organizational structure. In every
instance, it will be a matter of ensuring that those selected are exactly
those who give the final list of organizational core values the authority to
gain footing, build traction, and gain momentum.

Legal ownership of the organization comes into play also. While public companies and those owned by joint-venture capitalists can increase
the complexity of the process, it's important to remember that reversing
the flow of the Chicago River wasn't easy; nor was it impossible. Eventually, getting legal approval was imperative.

Every owner, shareholder, and joint-venture capitalist should not only
be at the center of approving such a process, they should also be first in
demanding that core values are in play to build value.

Regardless of the size, structure, and type of organization, there is always a defined leader of an organization. That is precisely the person who must *personally and organizationally* embrace this process. Otherwise, it can cause collateral damage if it is seen as a hypocritical move by leadership.

As fair warning, it is better to do nothing than to do it without a leader's full and lasting ownership.

There is no such thing as a positive return on partial integrity. The only return on partial integrity is a significant cost—if not a total loss.

> **It is better to do nothing than to do it without a leader's full and lasting ownership.**

The effectiveness of this team is a very personal issue. The leader and the team assembled to look at organizational core values must first have fully invested themselves in doing the hard work of digging for and establishing their own set of personal core values. This puts them in a position to be far more equipped to lead the establishment of a set of organizational core values. Those who come into this process without the hard work of establishing their own set of personal core values are rarely prepared for the effort at all.

This prerequisite preparation changes three critical elements:

> **There is no such thing as a positive return on partial integrity.**

- How well they'll come to know each other
- How effective they'll work together
- How authentic and valuable the list of organizational core values will prove to be

It's a matter of flow. And a matter of personally experiencing the struggle, confusion, insights, wisdom, and eventually the clarity that come from digging for your own personal list. You simply arrive at the beginning of this process with a different perspective and the potential for a much more valuable answer.

While the leadership team tasked to work on the identification of organizational core values is engaged in something collective, it's important that they approach it very personally. It's also important that they come together with their own personal values fully engaged. It may prove to be the first real test of the value of their personal values!

[Naming Core Values]

This isn't a one-time meeting or an expensive getaway at a fancy resort. Much like working on your personal core values, it is likely a series of meetings spread over a defined period of time, along with a mixture of group meetings and individual reflection throughout the process. It could very well begin with two or three days off-site and end in a similar fashion. If so, these off-site gatherings would be more effective in isolated settings with virtually no distractions. Likewise, the gathering would prove less effective in resort-type settings with their constantly tempting activities. It won't work well mixed into the agenda of other competing priorities. Any distraction—work or play—will take away from the type of focus needed for this effort.

The careful planning of the process determines, in direct proportion, the quality of the outcome and the potential of where everything goes from there.

Just as we stated in looking at our personal values, the assembled team is not looking for aspirational desires or current conditions in establishing the list of organizational core values. They are looking to name the truth of who you are, collectively, as an organization.

Much like the process of discovering personal core values, this process begins as an exercise in brainstorming. It is different from the process of working on your own personal values; it is both easier and harder because there are others involved in the process!

It's important that this brainstorming process be facilitated and led by—you guessed it—*the leader*. This means you're giving your full engagement in every aspect of the dialogue. It's not just about engaging everyone in the process, but it's about the leader personally digging, probing, encouraging, questioning, and modeling so others can do the same.

This focus doesn't start with trying to capture the perfect words to name the values. It starts with authentic, genuine, honest, and sometimes gut-wrenching conversation that digs out the essence of what is at the core of the organization.

Values may be expressed in words, but those words are a description of something that goes much deeper—beliefs, commitments, and other nonnegotiables for which you are willing to pay a price because they help you thrive.

> This group is not searching for the essentials of what you are willing to live *by*; it is searching for the essence of what you are willing to live *for*.

This group is not searching for the essentials of what you are willing to live *by*; it is searching for the essence of what you are willing to live *for*. Understanding the difference will change the depth and nature of the conversation.

At this stage of the process, the discussion should not be about what is possible. It should be about trying to establish what is truthful. It's not about deciding who is right, but rather about discovering what is real.

Remember, this team should never forget that the organizational core values *are the business*. It's not a list to be hung on the wall and forgotten so the team can get back to business. They must be a constant reminder of what this group is willing to go back and live for!

[The Final Words]

Words do matter. Once the essence is collectively clear to all involved, it comes time to creatively work on the language of specific words. It's at this point that you may want to bring in some creative wordsmith talent to crystalize the essence of the team's insights and wisdom into language that is inspiring, empowering, and memorable. Words matter, so it's important that they stay completely true to the intended essence.

This is why it's critical that the nature of the value is crystal clear before the language is created. These words should forever carry a dose of emotion, a sense of clarity, and an invitation to accountability.

> The experience of your leaders' journey toward the final list of organizational core values is just as important as the final list itself.

As with establishing your personal core values, the experience of your leaders' journey toward the final list of organizational core values is just as important as the final list itself.

Personal core values aren't just personal. They are the fuel for not only owning and living organizational core values but being in a position and a mind-set to create them. Remember question 21 in our current condition assessment? This is your chance to be able to eventually answer it with a confident and resounding bigger YES!

6

The Value of Core Values

How much value core values deliver in the end is in direct
proportion to how much a leader values them in the beginning.

When I started becoming laser-focused on core values as a part of my overall writing and speaking on leadership, I quickly came to a sobering realization: We don't really value core values in business.

I know this seems a bit harsh, but it also seems there are a number of other things we have come to really value in business: strategy, vision, mission, measurements, metrics, skills, and behaviors, among many other *things*. But core values aren't really among those things. We might talk about how core values are important to have, but I'm talking about *really valuing* them.

We really value all these *other* things. We've talked about them frequently. We've referenced them constantly, measured them regularly, and held them high. They've been used as a mantra. They've almost been used as a theology all their own—with their own commandments of sorts.

> **We don't really value core values in business.**

This led me to wonder if we truly understood the value of core values. It led me to believe that leaders needed to investigate the whole idea. It's hard to value something if you don't really know whether it actually brings value.

I proposed that for any leader to truly value core values, they first had to investigate and answer a very simple but defining question: Do you believe values build value?

> ## Do you believe values build value?

I suggested it was important for the investigation to precede the answer. I wasn't looking for an immediate gut-feeling answer to the question. I was looking for an informed, well-thought-out, intellectual decision. I was looking for the kind of answer a leader could stand by, live for, and find value within.

I challenged leaders to take on thirty days of investigation and introspection. I invited them to use every ounce of cognitive and analytical ability they could muster to determine whether core values added real value to their business or not. I encouraged them to draw on prior experiences as reference points using real-life examples. Most importantly, I asked them to notice over the following thirty days (in meetings, challenges, decisions, and relationships) whether core values might make a difference, and whether they could bring real value in every aspect of their business life.

I wasn't looking for them to come to the right answer. *I was looking for them to make a decision.* I asked them to let this same question wash over them at least once a day, every day, for those thirty days: Do I believe values build value? I requested that for thirty days, the answer simply be—*maybe*. Maybe they do and maybe they don't. I then instructed them to come to one of two answers on the thirty-first day—either *yes* or *no*.

I challenge you to answer the same question. *Do I believe values build value?* It's a great question to ponder as you are busy digging for your own core values. It is a question deserving of both an intellectual and emotional analysis.

I told those leaders they had to be willing to own whatever answer they chose—because their answer would own them. It would define their leadership. It will define your leadership too.

Moving from Getting to Receiving

As I continued my journey as a national speaker and author on leadership, it became more and more clear to me that little mattered in the skills of leadership if the leaders weren't fueled by a strong set of first personal, and then organizational, core values.

I fully embraced what was becoming clear to me, but certainly felt reservations about whether high-performing executives under large amounts of pressure were going to digest such a message. I knew there would be a lot of unpredictable elements—beginning with the "big dig" I would ask them to personally embark upon. I knew there would be great doses of uncertainty. I also knew there were some things I could predict.

In an executive's world of metrics, measurements, and a sometimes clouded sense of stewardship, I knew many a top executive would ask the inevitable question: "If I'm investing time, effort, and resources into all of this, then what am I going to get?" Ironically, loaded into their question was an inquiry about their ROI: their return on *investment*.

I knew there was an inherent problem that they would never see. It was embedded in the question of *getting*. It was a problem I certainly hadn't seen from the beginning. It was one I'd come to know from the questions executives asked.

Although I would eventually come to know it was the wrong question, to this day I still feel it's a fair question to ask. And in many ways it's a great place to start.

Organizations, depending on their size, spend hundreds, thousands, or even millions of dollars in three distinct areas: alignment, engagement, and service. There is little argument among high-performing executives that each of these three areas will make an impact on the bottom line. Most would agree there is a return on investment that comes from investing in these areas. They may not agree on how much return, but most would agree there is a return. I don't know of any executive who would honestly desire misalignment, disengaged employees, or a continuous delivery of bad service to their customers or clients. This is why hundreds, thousands, or millions of dollars are invested. Unfortunately, they are invested in the wrong way!

I'm not a big fan of silk flowers. I prefer the real thing. Our neighbors across the street have the most beautiful gardens. Every spring, summer, and fall, their gardens are filled with an ever-changing variety of the real thing.

There is not a silk flower in sight—because they don't invest in silk flowers. They don't go and *get* what they are really waiting for: real flowers. They invest in bulbs and seeds. They garden with care, and they *receive* an incredible garden.

We invest an awful lot of resources in expensive "silk flowers," and so what we get is the fake version of the real thing. Fake alignment. Fake engagement. Fake service. We get *expensive* fake alignment, engagement, and service.

We invest with good intentions, but in the wrong way. We sell out when we could be cultivating and harvesting the real thing. And the last time I checked, the "real thing" is always valued at a whole lot more than the fake.

Intentionally discovered personal and organizational core values are the bulbs and seeds. You won't *get* silk flowers from them. Over time you will *receive* natural alignment, authentic engagement, and genuine service.

[Natural Alignment]

When we think of organizational alignment, we are most often referring to alignment with a vision, mission, strategy, or goals. It usually isn't about alignment as much as asking if everyone is in line—on the same page. It's about *getting* aligned.

Alignment is a good thing, but how you get people there vs. how people arrive there are two very different value propositions.

Silk flower alignment cultivates false positioning and posturing, spinning of stories and measurements, and—worst of all—meetings after the meetings. Looking like a flower and being a flower are very different things. Looking aligned and being aligned are two significantly different value propositions. It's about moving from honoring the call to "get aligned" to honestly being aligned.

Alignment doesn't begin with vision, mission, strategy, or measurements. At least, *natural alignment* doesn't begin there. It begins with the alignment of personal and organizational core values. If those values are in alignment and in play, there is a natural alignment that evolves from there.

This critical alignment of values provides the context to see where there is misalignment between organizational core values and the mission, vision, and measurements of the organization. When those organizational values are known and intentionally lived every day, there is also clarity in which to see when mission, vision, and measurements are creating a drift away from those values.

The essence and intentional wording of the organizational core values give a common language with which to discuss any misalignment. Those same core values also provide the courage to have a discussion with anyone, at any time, regarding a perceived misalignment within the organization.

More importantly, the essence and intentional wording of the organizational values give the common language to intentionally create mission, vision, and measurements that are aligned in the first place.

By definition, if people have found the intersection of their personal values and the organization's values, and the organization's values have directed the alignment of mission, vision, and measurements, then people don't have to be brought into line. They will bring themselves into alignment.

You won't need to spin messages or hold expensive sessions to coerce people into alignment. They will already see the alignment and will likely let you know if there is misalignment. While executives might try to execute an alignment initiative, leaders don't. Leaders cultivate a set of values that allows everyone to embrace their responsibility to align themselves.

[Authentic Engagement]

Once personal and organizational core values are aligned, your efforts can go into being sure the mission, vision, and measurements stay aligned with the values. When they do, you are nurturing authentic engagement.

We treat engagement as a choice—as a decision. We can make a choice to temporarily engage, and we create circumstances that will temporarily engage others. The problem is that it is only temporary, and temporary engagement is expensive to maintain. Once again, we do something to get something. *Getting* can be very costly.

Employee engagement has become a big business. A lot of it is in the business of *getting* employees engaged. Well-timed, carefully worded employee engagement surveys can deliver a momentary measurement of engagement. It's like going to buy a silk flower arrangement of engagement.

Money can't buy or get *authentic engagement*. We can only buy manufactured engagement. There is only one brand of authentic engagement. It's the engagement found at the intentional intersection of personal and organizational core values.

Executives can't *get* employees engaged. For that matter, employees can't *get* themselves engaged. Engagement is an experience that is *received* when personal values and organizational values align. Aligning personal and organizational core values is the *leading indicator* that allows you to *receive* authentic engagement both personally and organizationally. Authentic engagement (leaders, executives, management, and employees alike) is simply a lagging indicator. Leading indicators are what unleash the momentum. Lagging indicators are the resulting value derived by our investment in the leading indicator. When we try to directly "purchase" a lagging indicator, we get the silk version.

This alignment of personal and organizational core values leads to authentic engagement defined by a peace and presence that enables a better and more consistent performance. It also leads to a natural retention of those employees who are meant to stay! Core values will serve you well in finding and sustaining your zone of authentic engagement. In serving you well, they also equip you to serve others well.

> This alignment of personal and organizational core values leads to authentic engagement.

[Genuine Service]

Service is not a methodology. Service methodologies work well for machines. A mechanical form of service works well in an ATM or on a well-thought-out website. But it doesn't work well for humans unless, of course, you want to turn them into robots, which is precisely what we have done to "service" in many organizations. We have streamlined and time-lined the service proposition. There is nothing genuine about it. Efficient on the surface? Maybe. Effective? Rarely. I call this "servicizing"—the mechanical form of service!

I'm amazed at how much we notice a genuine moment of great service. Some can't remember the last time they received genuine service because it's been so long. Others remember it clearly because it's so rare.

> **Genuine service is not a duty; it is an opportunity.**

Genuine service is not a process. It's an expression of both personal and organizational core values. Genuine service is not a duty; it is an opportunity. It's not a commodity; it's a connection.

Ironically, the person served most by providing genuine service is the person providing the service, because it nourishes a deeper sense of authentic engagement. It becomes quite a systematic and synergistic process!

Silk flower alignment and silk flower engagement are empty enough. But there is nothing more slick or empty than silk flower service. There is nothing valuable or genuine about it. There is only one thing that creates and provides genuine service: *core values.*

Moving Away from Reliance on Compliance

Today's cost of regulation, and its resultant compliance, is staggering. If you want to witness big business, look at the myriad of consulting services whose sole purpose is to help organizations manage compliance with an ever-increasing number of regulations.

We used to hold things out there and question them. That was the spirit of conversations on almost any front porch. A question didn't have to be 140 characters long or posted on social media. It was a conversation. Just being in the conversation was enough because the conversation got you thinking. And thinking drives awareness. Awareness opens the door to seeing things you've missed. It presents the possibility of seeing things in ways that are new—or so long forgotten that they have the potential to become new again.

Those conversations weren't about proving who was right or wrong.

They were not aimed at each other. They were aimed at the issue at hand, the issues you were holding out there.

In today's world, sometimes the questions themselves can be bombarded with criticism before the conversation ever begins. This is especially true when you call into question that a "good" thing may have negative attributes. Like our reliance on compliance!

Could it be possible that the degree of regulation needed in an organization (as large as a nation or corporation, or as small as an entrepreneurial adventure or a family) is in direct proportion to the depth, or lack of it, that the organization embraces and engages core values individually and collectively? Regulations multiply in the midst of a void of values.

Making regulations must be easier than inspiring core values.

Making regulations must be easier than inspiring core values.

Enforcement is more convenient. It can take less courage. It gives a follower—in a leadership position—something to execute rather than trying to become the leader who others would truly be inspired to follow. Allow me to push just a bit further!

You can never regulate yourself into greatness. Regulations have proven necessary, in some form or fashion, in almost any society. They come packaged in the form of laws, and federal and private contracts alike. Regulation adds complexity and steps to any process.

Then again, regulations may create order, they may force a change of direction, or they may provide protection. In some cases, they may create a common level of understanding. Sports provide a simple way to look at this. Every athletic event has rules and their own compliance officers called referees or umpires. In sports the rules, refs, and umps exist because players, coaches, and teams aren't wired or conditioned to call out their own violations of the spirit of the game.

We accept some level of need for verification, but we hate it when refs or umps start inserting themselves too far into the game. While it would be nice if players and teams called themselves out on a violation of a rule, it is probably not realistic to expect that. It would certainly change the experience. Picture a head coach blowing the whistle on his own player for being offside in a football game or calling a foul in a basketball game. Doesn't seem possible, does it? That's because there are very few professional athletic teams, college players, or coaches with a solid intentional grounding in their core. There will always be some measure of rules, regulations, or compliance. The question is how much or how many. We will likely never be fully free of the need for rules or regulations. It's more about ratio than riddance.

Regulations are even worse when they are intentionally or unintentionally used as a painkiller to mask the greater problem at hand. Just look to where regulations are deep, far, and wide, and you will likely see a direct correlation to the number of violations and a concurrent lack of connection to any level of real core values. And as a problem gets worse, we just pile on more regulations. Rarely does this work. It only creates a pattern of organizations putting creative energy into getting around the regulations rather than connecting deeper into their core.

> **Just look to where regulations are deep, far, and wide, and you will likely see a direct correlation to the number of violations and a concurrent lack of connection to any level of real core values.**

While necessary, regulations are rarely wanted—unless, of course, we are regulating someone else. We generally strive for regulations that have a more direct impact on others than ourselves. That thought alone may be worth self-reflection!

But I think we would be hard-pressed to find cases where regulations inspire anyone or anything to greatness. Regulations create limitations and expectations—but rarely motivation and inspiration. Almost without exception, regulations hold things back rather than propel things forward.

That changes a bit when it comes to self-regulation or the regulation initiated by our own choice. Regulations prevent what we are trying to avoid rather than what we are striving to achieve, or longing to be.

I'm not proposing the elimination of rules and regulations. I'm just raising some questions. Why do we put so much energy into regulations and so little effort into investigating, indicating, and integrating core values?

It seems to me that when a country or a company spends billions of dollars on the creation and enforcement of regulations, it's fair to ask a few questions. It seems fair to wonder if we've completely missed an impactful and untapped resource that could not only save us billions of dollars but in fact inspire the creation of billions more. What is more inspiring—elimination or creation? Regulations, by design, eliminate what we don't want. Core values, by design, create who and what we truly want to be.

Again, I'm not advocating simply eliminating rules and regulations. We have tried that before with undesirable results. It's obvious that they are needed. Rarely do you eliminate the need for something simply by getting rid of it. That can leave a dangerous void. It's far more profound to create something that ultimately makes whatever you want to eliminate no longer necessary. Ironically, by the way, trying to eliminate "that which eliminates" is a bit contradictory! It is far more about discovering a relational correlation.

It is precisely the relationship of core values and regulations.

The question really comes down to what you are relying on. Is it a reliance on compliance or a reliance on core values? Don't you think it's a question worthy of a response? The superficial answer would be "both," yet a deeper reflection focuses on the proportional amounts of each.

I'm convinced that if we took all the resources invested in creating, maintaining, and enforcing regulations and all the organizational time spent on the consequent compliance . . . let's just say we could probably reverse the flow of a lot of rivers!

Undervaluing Values

If there is one clear way to underestimate the value of core values—or to devalue them altogether—it's by seeing them primarily as your insurance policy to prevent bad things from happening. There is no question that core values (personal and organizational) can prevent bad things from happening.

However, seeing core values in this light reduces them to another exercise in compliance, and minimizes them to a set of rules telling us how we are to behave. This is hard for a lot of executives to get their head around and is why they ask the question *What am I going to get from all this?* It's hard to see a lot of value in a list of values when they are treated like terms in an insurance policy. Only minimal value resides in using core values as prevention tools in keeping bad things from happening. The significantly greater value awaits within all the upside potential core values have to offer.

The bottom-line truth is that neither personal nor organizational values *get* you anything. In fact, they don't *give* you anything either. What they will do in amazing ways is *give back* all that you put into them and more. You will be amazed at what you receive.

It is there, and only there, that you find the greatest value in core values.

A Valuable Paradox: Core Values Will Never Deliver What You Set Out to Get

I understand why an executive would want to question the return on investment when focusing on core values. I want to stress the inherently self-destructive nature of continuing to focus on that transaction—of *using* core values to *get* something. Core values don't like being used. They like being lived. Core values will never deliver what you set out to get.

I was talking with the executive team of a major health-care system.

They were doing quite well in terms of patient experience evaluations, averaging 4.0 on a 5.0 scale. But they were not satisfied: first, because they were a high-performance organization striving for the best scores possible, and second, because the difference between a 4.0 and a 5.0 translated into millions of lost dollars in Medicare reimbursements. I have not necessarily listed the reasons in the order of their priority to the company.

> Core values don't like being used. They like being lived.

I was brought into conversation with their team because they had received extensive advice and methodologies from highly regarded health-care consultants and felt they had applied their recommendations with great care. They appreciated the consultants' advice and genuinely felt it had helped them achieve the average 4.0 rating. But they couldn't get beyond the 4.0 rating. One of the executives felt a conversation addressing personal and organizational core values was the missing piece of the discussion. He believed it would make a significant impact on the patients' experience in an authentic and genuine way. He had a clear vision into the potential of core values.

> Core values will never deliver what you set out to get.

I was excited about talking with this executive team and looking forward to all they could experience in a commitment to core values. We scheduled a conference call specifically around the CEO's schedule—a call the CEO ultimately failed to join. We proceeded anyway, although I knew the CEO's absence was a big red flag. I was convinced everyone else had noticed the red flag too.

The executive team seemed to be reasonably engaged in the conversation, but their questions reflected a "prove it to me" kind of mind-set. I tried to patiently (no pun intended) answer their probing but thoughtful questions. The questions continued to heighten my concern about their real motives. Then one of them asked, "How can you prove that focusing on core values will get us from a 4.0 to a 5.0 average patient experience rating?" I didn't need a reason to question their motives anymore. They were crystal clear.

I politely, yet pointedly, responded to the question: "While I have no doubt about the positive impact a focus on personal and organizational core values *could* have on patient experience, I do question if it will have an impact in this situation, where the real reason for the focus is about achieving an end result. Core values respond to your commitment to core values, not to being used as a vehicle to get something else."

Motives matter. It clearly wasn't a bad thing to want to improve patient experience. It's just that core values don't take kindly to being used. You must define them, embrace them, and completely live them.

You will ultimately need to come to your own answer to the question *Do values build value?* As you ponder your answer, keep digging for your own personal core values. It is not easy to keep digging, but I think you will find something very valuable personally and then organizationally.

I like how a leader at one of my client organizations phrased it: "Our commitment to core values has changed everything. It has changed the conversation!"

Core values have a way of doing just that. They're actually quite valuable.

7

Getting Ready

Ready, set, go starts with getting ready.
ROI starts with getting really ready!

Iknow I have been beating up the concept of *get* and *getting*. But as a leader, there is one thing you need to *get*: ready!

This will prove to be the longest, toughest, most vulnerable ride of your time as a leader. There won't even be a close second on your list. If you aren't ready before you begin, you won't last the distance. I'm warning you. It's a long road that has no end. However, once your time of leadership has come and gone, the journey and legacy of core values that you leave to your organization will be your greatest gift of all.

We are approaching the final section of *Return On Integrity*, "Destiny." It is a specific framework for you to use as a starting point to build a creative model that works for your organization.

Our first two sections, "Dilemma" and "Definition," were designed with only one purpose in mind: helping YOU get ready. It might be helpful to review a few key points as we near the starting gate:

1. **Ponder the dilemma.** What makes core values so difficult? What puts pressure on core values, both the good things and bad? You might want to review the "Boulders" section on page 16. While we have explored these at the macro level, it will be important for you to carefully consider the roadblocks at the micro level within your organization.

2. **Begin the process of defining your personal core values.** Get to clarity of your Version 1.0 list of your core values. Refer back to the "Getting Started: From 'How To' to 'I Do'" section on page 93. Use the *Values Brainstorming List* at http://www. BlumbergROI.com/tools or whatever other resource might help you introspectively dig to your core. This discovery of your personal core will continue to evolve as you lead others, but your Version 1.0 will put you in a position of readiness intellectually and emotionally in all you are getting ready to lead.

3. **Evaluate the current condition of your organization.** Be brutally honest in your assessment. Go back to the twenty-four-question assessment. This truth will be valuable in ensuring your readiness. See "Establishing Current Condition" on page 130.

4. **Think about your core team.** This will become especially important as you start to dig into establishing or reestablishing the core values of your organization. You will lead this team through all you have experienced in each of the steps above. The intentional selection of this team may rank second only to the intentional selections of your own personal core values. See "Establishing a Core Team" on page 134.

5. **Embrace and understand the value of core values.** This starts with the thirty-day-challenge question: *Do you believe values build value?* Throughout those thirty days, consider the details of Chapter 6 on *The Value of Core Values*. Use these ideas to stir

your creative thinking in seeing the specific potential of values creating value in your own organization. At the end of those thirty days, it is critical that you have come to an answer of *yes*. If still *maybe*, then perhaps you need a few more days, or you may need to invite others into a discussion—ideally, other CEOs. You will not be ready until the answer is truthfully *yes* within you. If ultimately your answer is *no*, then there is no reason to move forward. In fact, I would advise you not to proceed to the *Destiny* section. It will only cause you heartache, headache, wasted expenses, and a framework of hypocrisy. If your answer is *no*, do nothing further. As for *Return On Integrity*, consider yourself done! You can do what executives have done for decades: Execute with every skill you have and hope for the best. It has actually worked out for a few of them individually. For others, not so much. If, however, your answer is *yes*, let's keep moving! Just be sure you can explain this value of core values to others. I can tell you from experience, this is going to be harder than you think. *So be ready!*

With all of that, you are getting close to ready. Let's explore three more areas to be sure you are fully ready to lead your organization to a Return On Integrity.

A Capital Investment

It's important to understand that core values will cost you. This is true on a personal level and an organizational level. You have to be ready to "spend" on this investment. Spending will come in different forms. It will come in time, emotion, relationships, and yes, currency.

You have to be ready to spend. Remember two things: Not having core values will destroy you. And there is a *Return On Integrity*.

It's important that you think of this as a capital expenditure. Having started my career as a CPA, I must disclose that the taxing authorities won't let you account for it that way, but they can't control how you think about it. As defined by the taxing authorities, it is probably a fair accounting treatment because this "capital investment" isn't set up for depreciation. It is an investment that appreciates!

> **Not having core values will destroy you.**

Let your own personal values be your guide in how to "invest" wisely, efficiently, and effectively. But be prepared to spend as you would with any worthwhile capital investment.

Depending on your size and structure, plan for this to be a multi-year capital investment. Remember, it never ends. The biggest investment will be on the front end, while the continuing yearly investment will soon be dwarfed by your Return On Integrity!

Plan accordingly before you start. The more "ready" you are to begin, the more clarity you will have on making a "capital investment" worthy of the value you are planning to create.

> **There is a Return On Integrity.**

Just like any other capital investment . . . it is a *hard* expenditure.

Nothing Soft about It . . .

It was among the most successful classic advertising campaigns ever—and, of all things, it was about toilet paper! Mr. George Whipple became one of the most recognizable faces in America as this campaign ran on TV and in print from 1964 to 1985 for Procter & Gamble's Charmin tissue.

In the commercial, Mr. George Whipple stood next to the Charmin display in the grocery store, preventing customers from squeezing the irresistibly soft Charmin. As the "softness" police, he would scold the violators. But in the end (so to speak!), he himself could no longer resist squeezing. In doing so, the ad did a great job of selling softness. It worked well because, in selling the softness, it was selling the truth. Charmin was in fact "squeezably soft." And we bought it! We bought it because we saw the real value in the softness.

Unfortunately, over the past sixty years, a majority of leaders have seemed to buy into the idea that core values are squeezably soft. Not in a good way. Not in the way Mr. Whipple saw it. Core values have been seen as, you know, touchy-feely kind of stuff. We have failed to see the value in the softness. "Touchy-feely" soft in the business world is code for "less valuable."

This creates a huge dilemma, especially when nothing could be further from the truth! But it is the truth many executives have lived . . . core values are just the soft stuff.

As an organization grows and becomes increasingly complex, core values become more important, not less. They become the backbone, not the soft stuff. Nor are they easy. It takes meaningful cognitive and emotional soul-searching to establish not only the nonnegotiable but also the foundation that propels behavior, performance, internal and external relationships, creativity, purpose, fulfillment, and all else that drives a healthy organizational culture.

Core values, residing in the affective part of our mind, are emotional, but they are not soft. They eventually mold us. Not vice versa. Core values are not rigid, for they are the lifeblood flowing through every vein of an organization and every individual within it.

Many leaders will have to mentally unwind their prior experience of how organizations may have addressed core values. Our experience tells us what has been, but it can sometimes prevent us from seeing what could be. That can create a roadblock that keeps us from the truthful potential of the strategic capabilities that core values provide any leader.

A leader's prior negative experience had nothing to do with the truth about the strategic potential of core values. It had to do with the executive's inability to lead from his or her own core, and the inability to develop a culture inspired by the organization's intentional core values.

We have also evolved to a conventional wisdom that would suggest that actually living an organization's stated core values leads to soft decisions—or, at least, to avoiding the tough decisions. I'm not sure where this thinking comes from. In reality, core values require you to make the most difficult decisions.

Core values do not drive you to a nice decision. They drive you to the *right* decision. The nice decision is sometimes the wrong decision, and core values will guide you through making tough decisions, in a respectful way, with a thoughtful strategy to carry out that decision.

Until a leader's mind shifts from seeing core values as a "soft" issue to understanding their strategic potential, we face a terminal issue. You cannot lead what you do not embrace. You cannot embrace what you do not believe. And you cannot believe something—sometimes—until you are able to see it in a completely new way.

You need to get ready to reframe this perspective. It will be hard to do. It's been viewed, devalued, and relegated to softness for an awful long time. It will be your role, as a leader, to reestablish it from the inside out. Rather than reframing core values as something other than soft, you could take a Mr. Whipple approach of paradoxically selling the real value of the softness . . . or at least helping others genuinely see the value of core values!

No one can do this but you. The hard part won't be selling the idea. You can't *sell it*. The hard part will be in your initially *living it* so others can come to actually believe it. Remember, this will take time—patience and persistence. Everyone is used to silk flowers. Planting bulbs and seeds can get a little messy. Some will want to wait and see what will actually grow.

Embracing the softness sure seemed important when it came to something as critically and strategically important as toilet paper! Embracing core values is surely just as important.

For those who don't embrace core values, I'm sure Procter & Gamble would be more than glad to sell them plenty of rolls of irresistibly soft Charmin to clean up the eventual mess!

Changing a soft perspective can be really, really hard to do. Just get ready!

Resource Ready

Part of being ready is being resource ready. There are three particular groups that can play key roles on your team—Ambassadors, Human Resources, and Marketing. But this is not about delegation. You own this now and forever.

However, in organizations of almost any size, there are certain groups that can be extremely helpful in developing traction and momentum behind building value with core values.

Each group can lend a unique dimension that will stem from their identity and their talents. You don't need to go out to get *additional* resources; you need to build off the resources you already have—and in the process, you will enhance each of them.

[Ambassadors]

Ambassadors aren't a group per se, but they will surely become one. Simply put, Ambassadors are the people you can count on to live the focus on personal and organizational core values with the same level of commitment as you do.

This is not necessarily your formal top executive team. However, if it's not the majority of them, you will likely need to update your succession planning in the months ahead.

It is important for individuals to move along at their own pace. Authenticity is critical. Some on your executive team may need more time than others. The key is that they are moving at *some* pace. If not, there will come a time where you will need to consider moving them out. This assumes, of course, that you have used every personal and organizational value available to encourage those who are not moving or who are moving along at a slower pace than others. The quickest way of undermining or devaluing the value of core values is to allow a value virus to fester at the highest levels. Remember, there are times that core values require you to make very difficult decisions.

None of this "slower" group will be among your *first* Ambassadors. In the end, however, a number of them may very well become some of your *strongest* Ambassadors.

I hope you will be pleasantly surprised at just how many members of your top executive team will be eager to join you in embracing this initial stage of the process. It is critically important that they gravitate toward the Ambassador role naturally and are never prodded or made to feel guilty about not accepting the role.

It's important that you make the expectations clear. It's simple to clarify—it's the exact process you are putting yourself through. Through that process you will discover the current condition of your executive team and the potential leaders among them. It is through the same process that you will come to understand if they are potential Ambassador material right from the beginning.

The Ambassadors' role is simply to commit to intentionally living their personal core values 24/7 in all areas of their life, including home, work, and community. They will also commit to intentionally understanding, embracing, and living the organizational core values as those values are developed, and commit to proactively helping everyone around them do the same.

There are no Ambassador bonuses, accelerated pay, or promotion benefits—or any favoritism. Their Return On Integrity will be payment enough.

Your Ambassador team's heart will become stronger and stronger as the value of core values increases exponentially.

[Human Resources]

This next resource could be a tempting trap; not in and of itself, but because of conventional wisdom. The concept of values is a people issue, but you are *leading* an organizational strategy. *You* are the leader, and no other team or department is in charge. This is especially true when it comes to the human resources department.

If you want to slide back over to the softer side of things, then just delegate all of this to your human resources department. But they aren't likely to catch the baton when you throw it! They used to love being involved in core values, but they don't anymore. Not because of who they are, but because of who they have been programmed to be.

Many human resource professionals have washed their hands of core values. Not because they don't believe in them, but because it hasn't proven convenient to their careers. In an attempt to "get in alignment," many HR professionals turned their backs on the soft issues and on their colleagues who didn't follow suit. Grabbing on to the hard stuff was easier (and in their mind more strategic) than facing the truth about the strategic nature of core values. They opted to grasp for anything viewed to be the hard stuff in order to gain a seat at the executive table. It was shortsighted, because a "voice" at the table would have been much more effective.

Although my undergraduate degree in accounting equipped me for my eventual certification as a Certified Public Accountant, I ended up shifting my focus from numbers to people. Before launching my professional speaking career in 1996, I spent the majority of my time working in the world of human resource professionals. So I'm not coming at them. I loved being one of them. That's precisely why I'm sometimes hardest on them.

I've often asked audiences of HR professionals to look in the mirror and ask themselves the question *In reaching for success, have I sold my soul?* Unfortunately, many will vulnerably admit it's exactly what they did. Others have become too hardened—sitting slumped in their seat at the executive table—to even consider the question. Some have managed to remain courageous, and it would be ideal if you have one of them on your team. They will find it refreshing to find their core again. Once they do, they will become a great resource on your team.

Their role on your team will become increasingly important the further you move along in this journey. Core values, after all, are about people. Your human resource professionals provide a wonderful skill base to the process—and a necessary one—considering the demand your leadership will eventually make on various human capital strategies, such as sourcing, recruiting, assessment, performance reviews, career development, succession planning, and the evolution of a strong culture.

The subject of core values will be music to their ears. But while they will certainly be a critical resource in your orchestra, you will always remain the conductor!

[Marketing]

The marketing department can also become a tempting trap when it comes to developing the organizational core values and is why so many organizations develop a "core brand" rather than intentional organizational core values. Organizations can fall into traps of their own creation when they believe the catchy clichés of their in-house wordsmiths.

If, however, marketing professionals who are truly gifted with language can find the depth within themselves to grasp the meaning of building value with core values, they will bring tremendous benefit to expressing the essence of the organizational core values you are seeking.

The involvement of marketing is a two-way street. While you don't want your organizational core values to be created as a brand, you clearly want your brand to be an expression of your core values. Marketing's full involvement will significantly increase the odds that the brand is tightly aligned to the essence of the organizational core values. When that is the case, your brand will reflect a tapestry of who you are, what you do, and how you do it.

There is only one requirement of human resources and marketing: that they fully invest themselves in that same digging process, just like you and your leadership team. Finally, they need to be a natural part of your Ambassador group before they should contribute any of their human resources or marketing talent.

* * *

Notice I didn't request that you get fully prepared. I simply asked you to get ready. There is no way that you can be fully prepared for the journey that awaits you. If you waited to be fully prepared, you would never begin the journey. There are some aspects of preparation that you can only learn on the journey itself.

As a leader, you will likely remain only a few steps ahead of everyone else. A few steps ahead are all a leader needs. Remember, if you were too many steps ahead, they would lose sight of your leadership and all you are trying to lead. The journey is about to begin. *Are you ready?*

> **As a leader, you will likely remain only a few steps ahead of everyone else. A few steps ahead are all a leader needs. If you were too many steps ahead, they would lose sight of your leadership and all you are trying to lead.**

Section 3:

Destiny

This is where it gets exciting—and incredibly important.
Our focus, up to this point, has been on preparing you to lead a Return On Integrity. We have talked about the importance of your personal investment in digging for your personal core values. Having done so, you will be able to lead others to eventually make the same investment. While we think of each individual's initial investment as digging, the process of evolving a culture that builds a Return On Integrity is a collective journey.

This final section is much like the GPS for your journey. I call it the *Destiny Road Map*. Much like checking the road map routing on your GPS before you start driving, it's helpful to have a general feel for the overall routing before you start leading this journey. That will be our approach here.

I must admit I had mixed feelings about the approach of this section, or about even including it at all. My fear was of boxing in the potential of the process when my intent was simply to set forth a foundation to inspire your own process. Or worse yet, in a world that reveres methodologies and process, I was afraid this process would offer a convenient opportunity to grab on to the familiar reliance on structure and framework. It would be easy to react to a sense of urgency to just get going, and in doing so, miss the leader's critical, deeper dive of struggle, reflection, insights, and ultimate commitment that brings real value to this process.

*   *   *

It's the connection between a leader's commitment to values *and his commitment to action* that makes the process scalable and valuable to all.

I fully realize the framework for action will vary significantly as it's applied to organizations varying in size, geographic structure, governance, and ownership, and the current state of their culture. All of these must be factored into customizing the *Destiny Road Map* to be most effective in your environment. I would propose that you consider two points of caution as you contemplate your customization:

> • First, it would be easy to peruse the details of the *Destiny Road Map* and quickly jump to what you can't do, or what you think wouldn't work in your environment. Don't be quick to jump into a can't-do mind-set in your planning; never lose sight of the incredible potential awaiting as you build your Return On Integrity. You don't want to sell it short. I would encourage you to think in terms of creative possibilities. As you review the *Destiny Road Map* framework, think of everything you can do by bringing your leadership

Don't be quick to jump into a can't-do mind-set in your planning.

commitment alive in a very creative way. Your commitment will require a use of resources—both time and real dollars. At the same time, it will likely shine the light on opportunities where you can eliminate other uses of time and real dollars that currently waste resources. Find where you can reallocate resources to realize a more robust ROI—a Return On Integrity and a return on investment.

* Second, some organizations may *feel* great about their current culture. Many factors can influence how we feel about the culture, including a facade of brilliant branding, a superficial lineup of expensive employee events, a currently relevant hot product or service, a robust bottom line, or the current perception that it's a great place to work. All of these extras are great to have, yet they can potentially cause a huge dilemma and prevent you from fully embracing the substance of your journey ahead. All of these extras are temporary situations, and core values are not situational. They are trajectory. Some of today's most successful companies could find themselves falling into the trap of thinking they are infallible. A sense of infallibility can exist in a major corporation or a highly successful entrepreneurial adventure. But situations change. Just look at Kodak, Sears, or Arthur Andersen. Great success is a situation that can color the facade of a culture, but it isn't guaranteed to last. Don't let the current perception of your culture shortcut your efforts in

> ## Core values are not situational. They are trajectory.

planning your *Destiny Road Map*. And don't let others shortcut it for you. Perception of culture is a poor substitute for the far more accurate process of assessing your organization's "current condition" that we discussed in Chapter 5.

With all that in mind, let's take a look at the anticipated routing along your *Destiny Road Map*.

[The *Destiny Road Map*]

This *Destiny Road Map* is about one thing: an intentional commitment to personal and organizational core values. Everything flows from there. The road map is divided into four interconnected phases:

- Reboot and Reset
- Reveal and Refine
- Resonate and Remind
- Reinforce and Reenergize

Each phase has its own focus, characteristics, and purpose. Yet, none of them stand alone. They are interdependent segments of the same journey.

All of them represent a season of time to guide you forward. There are no preplanned repeating cycles, although you will certainly feel there are as you take two steps forward and one step back. And there will certainly be times when you feel like it's one step forward and two steps back. On those days, just know you are having a bad case of normal. Also know, with your personal commitment, that it's a one-way journey that will keep getting richer and more rewarding along the way. You can easily stage the four phases as one phase per quarter. You can also let the process breathe and conduct the stages over a period of sixteen to twenty months. Whatever schedule you decide on, it's preferable to set up the entire schedule at the beginning.

Sample schedules might look something like this:

Sample schedules

Phase	12 months	16 months	20 months
Reboot and Reset	March	March	March
Small Team Meeting #1	May	June	July
Reveal and Refine	July	August	November
Small Team Meeting #2	September	October	January
Resonate and Remind	November	January	March
Small Team Meeting #3	January	April	July
Reinforce and Reenergize	March	June	October

Over the course of the next four chapters, we will take an individual look at each phase. Each chapter will address four aspects of the particular phase:

- **Overview**—an introduction to the phase
- **Preparation**—your planning for the phase
- **Gatherings**—Large Group Sessions, Ambassador Meetings, and Small Team Meetings
- **Emphasis and Challenges**—unique aspects of the phase

As we begin down this road, I'm reminded of the sentiments of author Scott Peck and the words of Robert Frost—unfortunately, it's a road less traveled. The road map that follows will differentiate executives who claim values are important from leaders who are willing to take that road themselves and lead others there, too.

*   *   *

At the end of your journey, you will look back. *We all will.* It is from there that you will see your greatest ROI—your Return On Integrity.

Let the journey begin!

8

Reboot and Reset

While meaningful change happens over a period of time,
it begins in a defining moment.

Traveling along the *Destiny Road Map* is a journey that never ends—*yet it has only one beginning.* You get only one chance to start for the first time. You can start over again for the second or third time, but that comes with significant challenges.

The great news is, this is your first time to step into leading everyone along the *Destiny Road Map.*

This first phase is unique. It's not a span of time; it's a moment in time. It's the critical beginning. Everything we have been exploring up to this point is a prequel of each of the phases to come. I think of this *Prequel Phase* as the critical on-ramp to your four-part journey of the *Destiny Road Map.*

All of it has been preparing you for this first phase of the collective journey—*Reboot and Reset.*

It's important that your *Reboot and Reset* is not perceived, communicated, or experienced as the grand rollout of just another new initiative.

It has to be understood as a defined new beginning. It's crucial that every-one experiences it as *a line in the sand*.

It's a moment that separates the past from the future. While it clearly isn't about turning your back on the past, it is about turning over a new leaf. While much will be discovered in the months ahead, only one thing needs to be made clear in this moment: your genuine and authentic com-mitment to personal and organizational core values. You can make it clear you don't have all the answers, for you won't! You are just setting the direction and the trajectory forward.

Preparation

There's only one factor that determines the timing of your *Reboot and Reset*: The moment your own personal commitment is real. Only you can know if and when it's real.

[The Leader's Commitment]

You won't *decide* if your commitment is real. You'll emotionally *realize* it has become real to you through the discovery of your personal core values and your exploration of and conclusion about the real value core values can bring.

The launch moment of *Reboot and Reset* should never be planned until you have fully realized this commitment is *real* to you. Remember, you only get a "first chance" at a *Reboot and Reset* one time. So don't fire a blank with a false or uncertain commitment. This is one hard and fast rule: Don't move forward until you know your commitment is personal and it's real. It's at that point, and only from there, that you'll be ready to lead yourself and others to a Return On Integrity. And you are the only one who can effectively lead it. So if YOU are not ready, *wait.*

While this personal and private commitment is cultivated deep within you, it's the centerpiece of what goes public in *Reboot and Reset*. In fact, the entire *Reboot and Reset* centers on you.

It is the story of your own *Reboot and Reset*. It's a story more personal than you have likely ever shared in your role as a leader. It's a story of vulnerability, reflection, discovery, learning, and—the commitment you found in the midst of it all. It's your personal story shared in a way that looks back to where you've been, pointedly recognizes where you are, and brings insight into how you plan to lead everyone forward. It will likely feel different from anything your people have experienced before. And maybe different from anything you have ever done before.

It's a story, shared as a gift, to lead everyone else to their own story. It's expressed with one thing in mind: clarity about commitment to the core.

All you have to share at this point are words within your revealing story. Trust me, it will be enough. The action to follow in the months ahead will bring every word of it to life.

[The Prequel Phase]

Before we officially move forward drawing a "line in the sand" of *Reboot and Reset*, it would be helpful to do a quick review of everything that has come before—what we have now termed the *Prequel Phase*. Hopefully, a review of each of the following will provide you a gut-check to see how ready you are to lead the journey. It is important that you have not only completed each of these prequel steps but have proactively reflected on your experience with each of them.

1. **Ponder the dilemma.** What makes core values so difficult? What puts pressure on core values? What are the good things and the bad? It brings a realistic context to the challenge and opportunity ahead.

2. **Dig for your personal core values.** The experience of this personal introspection may be the most powerful insight you share. The experience of your own personal digging will also be the nucleus of what earns you the right to lead. At this point you may only have a solid Version 1.0 of Core Values. Sharing the fact that you are still discovering will bring credibility to your commitment.

3. **Embrace and understand the value of core values.** Remember the thirty-day-challenge question: "Do you believe values build value?" This experience will also make for an insightful sharing in your *Reboot and Reset* story. I can only assume you wouldn't be moving forward with a *Reboot and Reset* if you hadn't arrived at a "*yes*" answer to this question. The journey of your thirty days of "*maybe*" will also make for good content to your *Reboot and Reset* story! Revisit that experience and make note of what insights you noted that will be relevant to share.

4. **Determine the current condition of your organization.** As we said before, be brutally honest in your assessment and forthcoming in how you plan to share it. The current condition sits right on top of the line in the sand. It's an excellent time to expose which core values are veneer and which are deeply known, understood, embraced, and lived by all.

5. **Lead your leadership team.** By the time you get to *Reboot and Reset*, you will have done the four things above. It's imperative that the majority of your leadership team has found the same level of personal commitment as you. Not everyone will be at that point. That's just fine. It's important that the commitment is real and that individuals are not just getting into line. It's important that everyone on the team understands where each member of the team stands on commitment. It's your role to make it safe for each leader to share the truth. How this team is coming along

may influence your decision as to the exact timing of your *Reboot and Reset*. It may be a time well beyond your arrival at your own personal commitment.

[Building Your Story]

Each segment of the *Prequel Phase* is designed specifically to create an experience for you. When it comes to core values, it's impossible to lead what you haven't fully experienced yourself. The *Prequel Phase* is not about getting ready for the *Reboot and Reset*. The *Prequel Phase* is about getting YOU ready. If you arrive at a genuine commitment, there will be a story to be told.

Your story won't be fully understood until you look back across the landscape of your entire *Prequel Phase* experience. It will, however, be helpful to capture a number of notes along the way. These notes will be priceless nuggets of content that will help you see your story as you look back over your shoulder. To capture these notes, I would highly recommend you purchase some form of a new journal. Mark it as your *Prequel Phase* journal. It will be a great place to capture all of your thoughts, details, insights, wisdom, and the evolution of your personal core values. It will likely become a reference point for years to come. It will also be the point of departure where you document the adventure of the entire process, eventually moving from your stories to the stories of others.

You may have never kept a journal before, or it may not be your thing. This time, it's a must. Your notes may be pages of paragraphs, notes in outline form or in the form of a mind map, or may simply be pictures or doodling. However you document the experience, it's important you capture the details along the way, details of the content reflecting your thoughts on each segment of the *Prequel Phase* as well as details of where you were (date, time, place, setting, season, weather) and how you felt. Those feelings may cover a wide range of emotions, some the total opposite of the others. Capture anything and everything that catches your attention. At the end of each personal session, take three minutes to capture anything you missed—what you didn't see, what might have been between the lines of that specific experience.

Your experience will be unique, and so will your story.

Don't think you will remember the nuances of your *Prequel Phase*. Capture them as you go, as you experience them, never giving any thought about how any of it will fit into your *Reboot and Reset* story. It will only be in looking back that you will understand what is relevant to bring forward into your story of genuine commitment to personal and organizational core values. It will be important for you to fully draw upon your experience and your journal notes that remind you of the memorable details. It will also be important for you to understand and draw upon the gift of story itself.

Story is the oldest form of communication in the human race. It's the most personal, powerful, and memorable form of communication. It is also a gift you give to those who listen.

Reboot and Reset is about YOUR story, but it's not about YOU. It is about you giving others the chance to begin their story. It's your invitation— and the story allows you to show them, not tell them.

We could dedicate an entire section on "story," or fill an entire book. For your *Reboot and Reset,* I think the following key points will be just what you need:

- **Lay out the details of your experience.** Think back over what actually happened. Think of times on your calendar, places you reflected, conversations you had with others and with yourself. Simply document each of the times and places you engaged in your *Prequel Phase* experience. This list includes what took place even prior to the *Prequel Phase*—specific incidents growing up that impacted your experience with core values, incidents that reflect a prior experience with values in business, and conversations or incidents that stirred your thinking about values. Somehow and somewhere along the way, you connected with this book. How did that happen? Then think of each and every time you sat down for another installment of your *Prequel Phase*. Don't filter or prioritize this list. Just capture the true and tangible moments you remember. Each of these real events is a possible chapter in your story. Think of this as no more than listing out the pieces of the story.

- **Review the list of events, creating a sequence, and then begin to link and layer your story.** This involves connecting the dots and adding the details. This is where your journal notes will prove priceless. Think of your story as a freight train with a few cars on it. Each scene of your story is one of the freight cars. Trains work because each car is *connected* to the other. Each car or, in your case, each scene pulls the other one along. You will want to sequence your story in a way that takes your audience on a logical ride along your experience. You will want to *tell* your story, not *tell about* your story. You do this by creating the scene and *bringing your audience into the scene* with the details you describe: who, what, when, where, and why. This is not a presentation. *It's a story.* Stories have scenes, and scenes can be brought into 3-D by words and pictures. Consider whether actual pictures in slides add to the experience. Just be sure you don't create a PowerPoint presentation! Each segment will reveal thoughts, ideas, wisdom, and a few interesting details that allow the audience to *come into your story.* Layering your story gives you the freedom to add all the details you can remember, or that your journal can provide you! At this point, the more details—of every aspect—the better.

- **Limit and lighten your story.** This is critical. Think of it as putting your story on a diet. Now that you have layered it up, we can become more selective about which scenes and the details of each of those scenes matter the most. This is where you look through the eyes of your audience and decide which details will serve them the best. Remember, this is not about you. It's about them. You will take your story and begin to craft it with great intention by removing what is not necessary and clinging to what is relevant. The French author Antoine de Saint-Exupéry captured this notion exquisitely when he said, "Perfection is achieved not when there is nothing more to add, but when there is nothing left to take away." Limit and lighten your story to perfection!

- **Rehearse your story again and again.** Your rehearsals are a critical part of your getting ready. This is not a rehearsal in the theater of your mind. The rehearsal in the theater of your mind is where you sit and THINK about what you are going to do and say. You rehearse it in your mind, but you never actually do it! I'm talking about a REAL rehearsal, actually doing it again and again—out loud. You will want to rehearse as if this rehearsal room were filled with the number of people to whom you will be speaking at your *Reboot and Reset.* You will want to use full volume in your voice. This out-loud rehearsal will reveal how your story fits together and how effectively you deliver the words you choose. As you practice, think of three important aspects of your voice: volume (loud and soft), speed (fast and slow), and your variation of those two aspects. These rehearsals are not about delivering with perfection; they are about allowing you to be genuine and free in the moment of your real delivery.

Your story will be the centerpiece of *Reboot and Reset.* I love the opportunity to be invited as the guest speaker at such sessions to bring focus to the foundational concepts of personal and organizational core values. I love it most when I'm simply the warmup act to the leader who is sharing his personal story. Nothing will make your *Reboot and*

Reset more powerful than your honest investment in the *Prequel Phase* of your journey. What you share in your story is the invitation for others to share theirs.

Gathering

Remember that *Reboot and Reset* is an event that takes place in a moment of time. It is your first Large Group Session of the journey. This event will vary in nature based on the specifics of your organization. There are numerous details and demographics that will impact the nature of your event. Remember that you only get one chance to *Reboot and Reset* for the first time. Just one time—this time—and you want to make it count forever.

[Planning the Session]

You should apply the highest standards when making decisions on where and how you are going to do this event.

The ideal approach is to hold this event one time, in one location, with every employee present, at the same time! While you may agree this scenario is ideal, you may also quickly be noting that it is nowhere close to being practical. Depending on the size and geographical makeup of your organization, that may very well be true. But don't dive to the lowest common denominator just yet.

Think creatively about what you could do without focusing on what you can't do. If in-person, at one time, in one location is simply impossible, then begin to break it down by level and then by location.

As the size of the organization scales larger, an in-person option may have to give way to technology. But the in-person impact on an experience so personal simply cannot be underestimated. It's enormous.

[Call to Action]

You have been getting ready for quite some time. *Reboot and Reset* is all about inviting everyone into the process. Through sharing your own *Reboot and Reset* story, you invite your audience into their story. In effect, you are inviting them into the next phase, *Reveal and Refine*. It's their own version of a prequel phase.

There are three prework assignments you will need to cover with them so they can prepare for·their first *Small Team Meeting*:

- They need to answer the following question: Do you believe core values build value?

- They need to start building their Version 1.0 of personal core values.

- They need to consider the potential and roadblocks to a culture driven by values.

That's it. At this point on the *Destiny Road Map*, that's all you need them to do and that's all you want them to do. Share with them the *Core Values Brainstorming List* at the following link: http://www.BlumbergROI.com/tools.

* * *

You may have noticed that the detailed steps of your *Prequel Phase* did not include any reference or work on establishing or reestablishing the organization's core values. That's because it's specifically and intentionally a post–*Reboot and Reset* activity.

The *Reboot and Reset* phase is about your personal story and the start of their personal journey of discovery. Any mention of organizational core values in this defining moment would derail their critical focus on personal core values. Remember, we would always prefer to discuss organizational core values rather than personal core values. Don't let your audience fall into the default trap of looking at the outside and judging others before they look on the inside.

Looking on the inside changes everything, including how everyone moves to the second phase, *Reveal and Refine*, on the outside.

Emphasis and Challenges

Drawing that line in the sand is the most critical moment within *Reboot and Reset*.

This line is about moving forward. The past is the past and can only be a burden, judgment, or excuse that weighs down the future. It doesn't mean that bad behavior will cease overnight. It just means that prior bad behavior can't be carried over the line.

This moment is a new beginning. Everyone gets a clean slate as they enter into their own prequel phase. The only exception would be if there has been any illegal or immoral behavior. Any such cases ideally should be addressed before you *Reboot and Reset* and draw your line in the sand.

I remember both learning and then teaching hundreds of professionals how to conduct a very effective framework of behavioral interviews. The premise of behavioral interviews (when properly conducted using strictly historical events) is that *past behavior is your best predictor of future performance*. I firmly believe that to be true—except when a line in the sand invites a person to investigate, discover, and embrace the personal values at their core. Most people have never gone to this core and therefore they do not know it, nor have they intentionally drawn from it. The line in the sand has the potential for changing everything—including future behaviors very different from those of the past!

The line in the sand quarantines the past while it sets the stage for the future. No matter what you do, no matter what story you tell, there will still be a large number of people in your audience chalking this up as another flavor of the month. There are two reasons this may happen. The first is past experiences with meetings and initiatives. The second is because it's really convenient. If they can justify this as a flavor of the month, they can assume it takes them off the hook for having to do anything—especially something like *Reveal and Refine*. It's important you make clear what this is NOT. It is not an initiative or flavor of the month. And then it's important you make clear what it IS! It is the way forward.

[The Way Forward]

From this point forward, everyone will be involved in some form of the current phase at hand. This defining moment is now history, and the next phase begins. Every phase moving forward is ideally an alternating combination of two types of gatherings:

- **Small Team Meetings.** These meetings are each led by one of your Ambassadors. This allows employees to engage in conversation and learn in smaller settings. It also allows you to equip and grow more leaders through the development of your Ambassador team.

- **Large Group Sessions.** Like your *Reboot and Reset* session, these gatherings are designed to pull everyone back together. They allow you and other members of your leadership team to address all employees with one message at one time in each of the phases of your *Destiny Road Map* journey.

> **Once again, do what you can do without concerning yourself with what you can't.**

Once again, do what you can do without concerning yourself with what you can't.

Reboot and Reset is an incredible opportunity. It is a defining moment. Make it awesome—and then let it become the least memorable moment by making everything that follows it even better!

9

Reveal and Refine

The birthplace of a Return On Integrity is precisely at the intersection of personal and organizational core values.

There are two key aspects to *Reveal and Refine*: One is scaling the focus on personal core values throughout the organization, and the other is initiating the focus on organizational core values.

The first aspect relates to the process of helping *everyone* in the organization define who they are through revealing and refining their own personal core values. You have made this part of your call to action in the *Reboot and Reset* session. Now the key becomes setting into motion the inspiration and accountability needed to make that actually happen.

The other aspect relates to your selected team helping you define who the organization is by establishing or reestablishing the organization's core values.

Very quickly, numerous aspects of this journey will be initiated. Hopefully, it will create an initial buzz that kicks everything into motion from a lot of different angles!

Preparation

This phase is focused on the simultaneous progression on four fronts:

- Gathering Ambassadors to lead Small Teams
- Conducting Small Team Meeting #1
- Establishing or reestablishing organizational core values
- Preparing for Large Group Session #2

This phase is critical for gaining traction on all fronts with everyone now involved in some capacity. It is here that scalability and broad-based traction take hold on numerous fronts. While these efforts run in parallel throughout the *Reveal and Refine* phase, they all come into focus by the Large Group Session that culminates in creating the intersection of personal and organizational core values. All of this hinges on the process becoming very personal for each and every employee.

[The Ambassador/Small Team Effect]

Remember the Ambassadors? Hopefully by now you have a number of them on your leadership team, at least the genuine leaders on your leadership team! These are the individuals who have *chosen* to commit to defining and living their personal core values 24/7 in all aspects of their life—work, home, and community. We need them for one more role: leading Small Team Meetings.

Like you, the Ambassadors are a few steps ahead of everyone else and will be in a position to guide and facilitate everyone else through the three call-to-action challenges you gave to all employees at the *Reboot and Reset* session:

- To answer: Do you believe core values build value?
- To start: Their own Version 1.0 of personal core values.

- To consider: The potential and roadblocks to a culture driven by values.

Small Team Meetings are groupings of no more than ten employees, if feasible. You can take a couple of different approaches in building these teams. You can create teams from natural groupings that already exist in current work teams or departments. You can also use this as an opportunity for employees to connect across work groups, meeting employees and building relationships with others they don't frequently interact with. This second approach allows ideas from various small teams to flow back into the current work teams or departments as participants come back together from a variety of Small Team Meetings.

In very large organizations, you may be faced with an approach involving different levels within the organization, and the process starts cascading downward. Small team size is critical in gaining relational traction at a personal, genuine level.

These hands-on sessions will bridge the momentum between each Large Group Session. Your Ambassadors are the glue to the process, so select your Small Team Leaders carefully. Not every Ambassador will be a Small Team Leader, but every Small Team Leader must be an Ambassador!

The key is that each Small Team Leader take full ownership of the experience created in their Small Team Meeting. The Large Group Sessions create momentum. The Small Team Meetings create individual ownership.

These meetings, of course, do not need to be held simultaneously. They should, however, be held within a defined range of time (say, within a certain four-week time frame) so you are keeping everyone at close to the same stage of the phase.

I have provided a Small Team Meeting sample agenda for each *Destiny Road Map* phase. These sample agendas are included under the "Small Team Meeting" header of each chapter.

[Ambassador Planning Sessions]

It's important the Ambassadors fully prepare for their assigned Small Team Meetings. The agendas are designed to be very streamlined and focused on the characteristics of the phase at hand.

While the Small Team Meetings aren't held simultaneously, it's important that they reflect consistency in the participants' experience across all of the Small Team Meetings. To ensure this consistency, it's important for all Ambassadors to meet together before each set of Small Team Meetings. It's critical that the Ambassador planning meeting be led by none other than you—the leader. This meeting should ideally be held in person, but if logistics don't allow for such a gathering, then an interactive webinar or conference call will suffice.

One objective of this first Ambassador planning meeting will be to ascertain if there has been any input since the *Reboot and Reset* Large Group Session that might fine-tune how the Ambassadors approach the proposed agenda. In the Ambassador planning meeting, you will want to take everyone through the Small Team Meeting agenda in specific detail. This will give everyone a chance to do real-time planning as well as be sure the process is collectively agreed upon as a group and individually understood among the Ambassadors. You should encourage both their input and ownership of the agenda. From that point forward, they should be well equipped to lead their Small Team Meeting #1. To ensure a common experience across all meetings, if an adjustment is proposed and agreed upon, it needs to be universal and noted in a revised agenda supplied to all Ambassadors.

Each Ambassador will need to take the responsibility for sending an email or electronic invitation stating the time, location, and required pre-work for their meeting. This will reinforce the participant call to action you already set forth in the *Reboot and Reset* session.

It might be helpful for you to share the level of attention and investment you personally gave in preparing for the *Reboot and Reset* session.

The Ambassadors must understand the importance of their role as they bring it down to a Small Team environment.

[Organizational Core Values Team]

While everyone is working on their personal core values, it's time to simultaneously begin clearly focusing on the core values of the organization. It's important to be very intentional as to who will be involved in this process. Refer back to "Establishing a Core Team," on page 134 to review criteria to consider for pulling together the right members to form an Organizational Core Values Team.

It's also important to assess how much time and effort you need/want to devote to a thoughtful establishment or reestablishment of the organizational core values. If you feel you are going to need more time than you have scheduled between the first and second Large Group plenary sessions, you may choose to begin this process before the *Reboot and Reset* phase and just keep this activity running in the background.

My experience has been that a reestablishment of the core values gives a fresh, current, and energized commitment to them. If the core values of your organization are long-standing pillars of the culture, you may want to continue to use those words with refreshed descriptions. If you do change previously stated core values, you will want to be intentional as you reveal the new values. You want to address how the previously stated values have either been rolled into newly described values or for some reason were not carried forward. You can point out that once previously stated values are more deeply understood, they can be revealed to be more of a need, want, or behavior. The key is to be intentional in addressing a new list of core values, whether that is a fresh new list, a revised list, or a recommitment to an old list.

You may also want to consider if it would be beneficial to gain input from managers and employees who may bring valuable insight, yet not be specifically selected to be on the Organizational Core Values Team. This could be either selective input from certain levels within the organization or a much broader net to capture ideas.

You will note the Small Team Meeting #1 agenda has a discussion point asking for input of ideas or words to consider in naming the organizational core values. While this may be beneficial in gaining a sense of ownership, the pros and cons should be considered. There's always the risk that input requested, but never used, can create disconnects. At the same time, there may be some incredible ideas suggested and the ideas not used could still be acknowledged at a subsequent Large Group Session. Some of those ideas may very well provide language that could be used in descriptions of core values. It's important to be intentional and consistent in this input process.

This discussion should embrace all the dynamics we defined in exploring your own personal core values. The discussions among the Organizational Core Value Team should be authentic, emotional discussions designed to reveal the truth—not current or aspirational conditions, but rather the truth of who the organization is and should be. It's important to also consider the differentiation of core values, needs, wants, and behaviors. We are striving, here, to define core values.

The organizational core values need to be discovered, considered, and embraced for approval by all appropriate parties before the next Large Group Session of *Reveal and Refine*. It's very important that you plan the start of this process so there is plenty of time to complete it by this next Large Group Session.

Gatherings

While this phase will likely include multiple meetings of the Organizational Core Values Team evolving the establishment or reestablishment of those values, the *Reveal and Refine* phase is highlighted with the first Small Team Meetings and the second Large Group Session.

[Small Team Meeting #1]

On the following page, you will see a draft agenda for Small Team Meeting #1. This agenda is designed simply as a guide for the Ambassador to lead the meeting. It is not designed for distribution to the participants.

Again, it's important that each Ambassador understand the flow of the agenda, their role in leading the meeting, their level of preparation needed and, ultimately, their need to embrace the agenda as their own.

Small Team Meeting #1:

REVEAL AND REFINE AGENDA

1. Welcome everyone.

2. Ambassador shares own personal story of their "prequel phase" discovery and abbreviated version of what the leader shared in the *Reboot and Reset* session, possibly asking some participants to share their own early experiences.

3. Lead group discussion on key question: *Do you believe core values build value?*

4. Brainstorm the possibilities participants see in a culture driven by strong organizational and personal core values. Then brainstorm roadblocks that can stand in the way.

5. Allow each participant to share ideas they currently have on their personal list of core values. It is ideal to have one participant give one idea and then move to the next participant and continue around the table four or five times providing one idea at a time. Encourage the group to listen carefully to the ideas of others and to consider those ideas as possibilities for their own list of core values.

6. Brainstorm some ideas the group members think would be helpful to consider as the leadership team takes a fresh look at the organizational core values.

7. Let the group know when the next Large Group Session will take place.

Facilitator Note: Remember, it's important to try to draw each person into the conversation so all participants are engaged in the discussion. It is often helpful to go around the table sequentially for input or to randomly call on individuals while being sure you have called on everyone. Your first meeting will likely be the most challenging. If you use this approach, however, the expectation will become clear that the engagement and input of everyone are important. You might even consider vocalizing this expectation in your welcoming comments at this first meeting.

[Reveal and Refine Large Group Session]

By now you should have momentum from the *Reboot and Reset* Large Group Session as well as from the more intimate structure of Small Team Meeting #1.

While the large group's *Reboot and Reset* moment-in-time, line-in-the-sand session was about sharing who *you* are through your story, this meeting is about sharing who the organization is through a draft set of the established or reestablished organizational core values.

Though the hallmark of this session is a focus on organizational core values, it is also a great opportunity to focus on the work individuals have done on their own core values. It would be ideal to be in a position where you could request all employees attending the Large Group Session bring their own personal core values with them. Hopefully, following their Small Team Meetings, they have made progress in coming to terms with their Version 1.0 set of core values. You may even want to have three or four people share their personal core values and their own journeys of discovery.

Eventually, however, the focus shifts to the organization. This is your chance to take the work of the Organizational Core Values Team you have called together and share it with everyone. While it's important for you to lead the effort, you may consider asking members of your team to take turns sharing the individual organizational core values in front of the large group. It will be important, however, for you to share your own commentary about each value as it is individually presented, or about each of them once they are revealed as a complete group.

Just the same as in sharing your story, your reflection on the creation of these core values—what they mean to you, what they mean to each participant listening, and what they mean to the organization as a whole—needs to be both personal and genuine. Consider how the concept of story could be used to bring each of the organizational core values to life. This is not a list of things. This is a revelation of who the organization chooses to be.

It is precisely at the intersection of an individual's personal core values and the core values of the organization where things begin to resonate!

Just as with personal values, the organizational core values being revealed are also a Version 1.0. It is important that you make this clear to give the flexibility for further refinement as needed in the short term. While the organizational core values are in their own refinement process, each employee will still be in a position to start considering how their personal core values connect and serve as fuel for bringing the organizational core values to life every day.

Emphasis and Challenges

While the process is still relatively fresh and new, it's also being pushed to a level of detail and challenge that is unprecedented in most organizations. Many in the organization may struggle with digging deep enough, or digging at all, to discover their core values. The foundation set in the first Small Team Meeting will be critical. It is important that Ambassadors are well grounded and willing to walk alongside those who are struggling with the process.

It's important for each Ambassador to make notations of challenges discovered along the way. The Ambassadors might want to establish an informal network or even establish "office hours" to assist one another as challenges arise. The level of expectations and accountability must be reflected through the quality of support you offer along the way.

As with any significant change, there will be the early adopters and then those who follow. Pay attention to the early adopters, for future leaders may very well be developing from that group!

We are setting the stage for core values to come to life. With personal values coming into focus and organizational core values being established, everyone has a chance to start trying it all out. Values need to become a common topic of discussion, and the language of those values should be frequently used in meetings, conversations, situations, and decisions where they either provide insight or are put to the test. At this stage, there will be many missteps along the way, and each will provide magnificent content for the teachable moments to come!

> **At this stage, there will be many missteps along the way, and each will provide magnificent content for the teachable moments to come!**

A new vision is being established by discovering personal core values and their intersection with the newly established or reestablished organizational values. This isn't a vision about where the organization is headed, but rather a fresh lens revealing who the organization really is.

At the moment your eyes are opened to the truth, you have automatically submitted to a new accountability, which can be very challenging personally and organizationally. Your awareness level will be significantly more focused. It's important that you instruct everyone else to focus their awareness on themselves and the inevitable evaluation that will come through that focus.

Everyone will have a lot on their plate as they try to put their own values into action every day while trying to engage the organizational values that have been set forth.

Expect some rough sailing through this phase and into the next. It's easy to become frustrated, and it's very human to want to help others with their corrections along the way. Not so fast! Encourage everyone to focus on themselves as they continue to reveal not only values, but how to refine them in a strategic way to capture all the potential that sits within those values. There will come a time when collective accountability, peer feedback, and eventually formal evaluations will become a broader form of development.

Remember, it's a journey that never ends.

10

Resonate and Remind

*There comes a time where we don't need to be taught
as much as we just need to be reminded.*

To prepare for full throttle ahead, it's important now to take note of how we are doing and where we have been:

- Personal core values have been identified and confirmed.
- The value of core values has been acknowledged.
- Both "roadblocks" and the "potential" of a values-driven culture have been identified.
- The organizational core values have been identified and revealed.

The mission of this phase will be to monitor the development of the areas listed above and to infuse clarity and encouragement where there is confusion.

* * *

Ultimately, behaviors are the expression of intentionally defined core values. In this phase, you will want to deepen the self-analysis on daily behaviors through much more tactical daily application and self-review.

Now it's time to prepare for Small Team Meeting #2. These meetings provide the critical opportunity for Ambassadors to take the pulse of individuals and note the common threads of progress and challenges within their group.

Just like before, you will want to conduct an Ambassador planning meeting to discuss the agenda, identify any relevant insights, and deal with any red flags that might indicate that an adjustment to the agenda is needed. These red flags might include someone still struggling with clarity on their own list of values or seeing how their personal core values help specifically fuel the organizational core values. Some red flags might be early signs of frustration in watching disconnects between the organizational core values and the lack of healthy behavioral changes. Many red flags are likely to surface. It is far better to surface them than to let them fester and infect the evolving culture. Ambassadors will need to know which red flags to handle within the Small Team Meetings and which to escalate for further attention. The process will, predictably, get messy from time to time along the journey.

The hallmark of this phase is the bridge from identification to application.

Preparation

The preparation for this phase will look familiar since it is simply moving along what is already in motion:

- Preparing Ambassadors for Small Team Meeting #2
- Refining organizational core values
- Preparing for the Large Group Session #3

The challenge will be the familiarity of it all. Don't fall into the trap of just going through the motions since everything is, in fact, in motion. The identification of values feels creative, fresh, and new. There can be a dangerous assumption that the process will just run itself from this point forward. This isn't the assumption we would have regarding a vision, mission, strategy, or methodology. Nor should it be when it comes to core values—personally or organizationally. Values build value with continued intentionality as we cross from identification to application.

The *Resonate and Remind* phase is where things get harder. You may see a very natural resistance starting to incubate. Application leads to personal and organizational accountability and this, of course, is never as fun as creating the values. This explains why core values have been seen as a soft topic, because we walk away from them as the process inevitably becomes difficult.

The key to leading this phase is keeping it fresh and evolving. You will soon see that on the other side of the bridge that takes you from identification to application is a wealth of incredible stories of application that will continue to keep it all fresh.

While crossing this bridge, you will look around and see just how challenging it can be to reverse the flow of the river—sometimes for others, but most often within ourselves.

[Preparing the Ambassadors]

The Ambassadors are especially critical to this phase in keeping momentum throughout the Small Team Meetings. It will be important that they see and feel your relentless commitment as the leader. When their momentum begins to waiver, they need to see your enthusiasm and commitment growing ever stronger. It is one thing to talk about the long-term nature of this process; it is another for the Ambassadors to start to experience it and then be able to turn around and share that experience with their Small Teams in a credible way.

So, preparation for Small Team Meeting #2 has as much to do with taking the pulse of the Ambassadors as it has to do with getting them mechanically ready to facilitate the agenda for their Small Team Meeting.

You can start by asking them what they see day to day *around* them: what is going well, what kind of questions they hear that reflect confusion, and where they see pushback or lack of initial buy-in.

It will then be important to ask the Ambassadors what they see day to day *within* themselves: what is going well; and what kind of questions stir internally that might reflect confusion, pushback, or lack of complete buy-in.

If it appears that all is great and wonderful, you haven't dug very deep.

Early on, you learned to dig to your personal core to reveal your values. In a similar fashion, here you will need to probe the discussion to move past the veneer of what they might perceive is safe for them to say. If it appears that all is great and wonderful, you haven't dug very deep.

Reversing the flow gets messy and can cause stress and discomfort. If you are not seeing, feeling, and experiencing this, you are still on the surface of the water. As any scuba diver will tell you, the beauty of it all is well beneath the surface. Dive deep for the truth. It will be inspiring for the Ambassadors to go there.

They will then be equipped to run their Small Team Meeting #2 and be in a position to credibly create the same experience for the participants in their meeting.

[Refining Organizational Core Values]

Now it's time to revisit the organizational core values. It is best to time this revisit after the Ambassadors have conducted their Small Team Meeting #2. That meeting's agenda will include a discussion on the rollout of the organizational core values. It will be important for members of your Organizational Core Values Team to solicit specific feedback from the Ambassadors' Small Team Meeting discussions. You may also want to get initial feedback from the Ambassadors themselves in the Ambassador planning meeting discussed above.

Again, as the leader, it is important that you lead this process and fully own the organizational core values. It is, however, also your chance to see what you can learn from the reveal. It will allow you to see things you wouldn't have noticed before and hear things that provide you a deeper insight. It is from there that you lead the Organizational Core Values Team to refine the narrative expression of the core values. In most cases, this refined version is the version set in stone—the stones of a foundation upon which every aspect of everything is built.

This process is more than just a revisit of the list. It is a very careful consideration of what was revealed and the wisdom that came from it. It may never be a perfect expression, but it can be an expression that brings incredible value. Refine it well.

[Preparing for Large Group Session #3]

Remember, the focus of this phase is the bridge walk from identification to application. Ultimately, this session is about nurturing accountability.

It will be important to set the stage for the challenges and expectations of accountability. While the benefits will be felt individually and collectively, accountability begins at a very individual and personal level.

As a leader, it would be helpful for you to be vulnerable enough to share your own initial challenges with "getting it right" all the time. The stumbles, missteps, and mishaps are all part of the walk across this bridge, and so is the honest awareness that comes from them.

It's one thing to share challenges, but it's quite another to provide tangible solutions. There are two very simple but powerful strategies for getting across the bridge and forever beyond it:

- Naming your Drift Catchers
- Establishing a PM/AM Examination

These two simple strategies, consistently applied, will ensure personal accountability, which in turn will create the consistent individual traction needed for sustaining collective momentum.

*   *   *

The first strategy is for everyone to enlist one or more "Drift Catchers." Catching our drift is very different from "getting our drift." Oftentimes in the midst of drifting, we subconsciously want to explain it away to ourselves and to others. It's like the old saying we have used—*you get my drift*—when we're frustrated and want someone to understand what we are trying to explain. In this case, what we need are people to catch our drift and bring us back! Remember the biggest dilemma of all: We don't go running away from core values. We go drifting away. And one day we wake up in a place we never meant to be. Drifting in a direction we never would have chosen.

> We don't go running away from core values. We go drifting away. And one day we wake up in a place we never meant to be. Drifting in a direction we never would have chosen.

We can take the chance that a courageous friend will happen to catch our drift, or we can proactively enlist some Drift Catchers. I would suggest the second approach. You specifically give three things to your Drift Catchers:

1. A list of your personal core values

2. A list of your organization's core values

3. The permission to tell you when you're drifting from either list

It's helpful to have at least one Drift Catcher outside the organization and one inside. Depending on your circumstances, you may want more than one in either setting. Their different vantage points give you an added advantage.

The bottom line is that your Drift Catcher is someone who loves you enough to tell you the truth—and I mean love exactly as I say it—and you love them enough to accept their truth, even when you don't want to hear what they are saying. If they love you, you may not want to hear what they are saying, but you definitely need to! You will also be more likely to truly listen.

It is crucial that you name your Drift Catchers well in advance of the third plenary session, since it will provide you the perfect opportunity to lead this strategy by example. You should explain how you selected your Drift Catchers and share their name and the role they play in your life.

You could even ask everyone in the audience to be your Drift Catcher! It would be an amazing symbol of boldness as a leader. They are going to be watching anyway, so you might as well benefit from it.

The Drift Catcher strategy can be powerful and useful in so many ways. There is plenty of research and conventional wisdom that supports the value in going public with goals, ambitions, and resolutions. There is also great value in going public with your core values. Yet, as powerful a strategy as it is, it still depends on others to respond to what they see in your behaviors and choices on the outside. Those behaviors and choices are also dependent on a sampling, because no matter who your Drift Catchers are, they are not with you 24/7.

* * *

A second strategy is guaranteed to make the role of your Drift Catchers much easier! It is the PM/AM Examination.

As in, every evening and every morning.

The PM element of this strategy focuses on the reinforcement of your personal core values. Think "P" for *personal.* It's important that you keep this brief because it's important that you keep it daily—seven days a week. The idea is simple. At the end of every day, possibly as you are putting your head on your pillow, review the various scenes of your day through the eyes of your personal core values. Think about the beginning of your day, and every person, meeting, challenge, and opportunity that followed. Review each one from three different vantage points:

1. Review those various scenes, noticing specifically where certain values came into play and really made a difference. It's important to notice where we get it right. This not only provides great encouragement and reinforcement, but we can learn how to become even more effective at bringing the value to life in future situations.

2. Review those same scenes again, except this time look for where one of your values would have been helpful, though you failed to draw on it. These are also great reminders and teachable moments that make us better the next time.

3. Finally, review your day in search of occasions where you might have violated one of your core values. This is not a process designed so you will beat yourself up over it. I'm sure you have a number of metrics and measurement tools you can use for that! This is simply a tool of awareness—noticing where we violate a value, how we feel about it, and what insight can be gleaned for future reference.

Each of these reviews can hold great wisdom for continuing to sharpen and strengthen our connection to our personal core.

The specific timing of this self-examination—just before falling asleep—is intentional. You will continue to process your awareness and related insights as you sleep. There is much published scientific research on the active and important functioning of the brain while we sleep. This research suggests that when you fall asleep, the brain wakes up to do its most important functions of processing and sorting. You might as well have it working on your core values too!

The AM segment of this two-part technique focuses on the organizational core values. Think of the "A" as *all* of us. This review allows you to be proactive in engaging the organizational core values. There is no doubt your schedule is busy and you have a natural sense of urgency in the early morning hours to get things started. You will want to limit this exercise to no more than five to seven minutes. Regardless of how busy your schedule might be, anyone can spare a few minutes. This is especially true when these minutes have the potential to return a hundredfold throughout the day, if not more!

This part of the technique has two segments:

1. Take the list and short narrative description (as applicable) of each organizational core value. Review just one value and description per day. The consistent commitment to this practice will have a cumulative impact of eventually embracing the entire list of values in a consistent way.

2. Look at your calendar for the day. This is an effective planning process to do anyway regardless of core values! The key here is to look at your schedule through the lens of the value you just reviewed and think how that value might play a positive impact on those scheduled items. Think in terms of the people involved in those activities, the relational challenges and investments, the topics involved, discussions to be had, and decisions to be made. How does the value upon which you are focused impact any

and/or all of them? What specific behaviors might that value intentionally put into action?

The PM/AM Examination structure is simple by design. But don't be fooled by this. It will be harder than you might think and more effective than you likely imagine. Its impact comes through your repetitive commitment to its simplicity.

*   *   *

The Drift Catcher and PM/AM Examination strategies are the focal point of the *Resonate and Remind* Large Group Session. It will be important for you and your Ambassadors to personally engage these strategies well in advance of this session. This will allow you to share these practices through the eyes of experience.

Start personally engaging in this daily practice on the evening following the *Reveal and Refine* Large Group Session This will give you a running start before the Ambassador Planning Meeting. You could share this practice (and your experience with it) at that meeting while challenging the Ambassadors to engage in the practice from that point forward. By the day of the *Resonate and Remind* Large Group Session, a number of you will have experience with it. You might consider having two or three Ambassadors share their personal experience of the "PM" portion of the examination and possibly two or three other Ambassadors share their personal experience of the "AM" portion.

As the Ambassadors complete their Small Team Meeting #2, they should provide any insights that are surfacing among the participants. Some of those insights might be unique to an individual, yet hold potential wisdom for all; and some of those insights may be more pervasive across numerous groups and provide a common theme you might want to specifically address. All of these insights give additional content you will likely want to share as everyone continues through this phase.

This Large Group Session should prove quite helpful to everyone as they continue to resonate with their individual role of creating a collective

Return On Integrity. It will also educate and encourage them about the value of reminders—their own daily reminders!

One last item for this Large Group Session #3 will be to begin foreshadowing the focus on the Return On Integrity being an unending focus. To "prime the pump" for our next phase, you might get the entire gathering to break into small groups of three participants each. Ask them to begin to brainstorm specific ways to individually and collectively keep alive an endless focus on core values and building an ever-increasing Return On Integrity. This will bring a high-energy close to the session as well as prepare everyone for their next Small Team Meeting. Encourage them to take notes and keep those notes handy!

With each passing Large Group Session, it will get increasingly tempting to add a lot of unrelated items to the agenda "while you have everyone all together." Avoid the temptation. You will want to just keep the main thing the main thing. You will want to keep the focus on values as the only thing—as everything!

Gatherings

So, again, you have three gatherings in this phase:

- Planning meeting with the Ambassadors
- Ambassadors' meeting with their Small Teams
- Everyone gathering for Large Group Session #3

By now there should be a rhythm to the process, but avoid the temptation to make anything routine—except your own daily PM/AM Examination!

We have thoroughly covered all you need to do for the Ambassador Meeting and the Large Group Session. The following Small Team Meeting #2 agenda should provide the details each Ambassador will need to prepare for facilitating their small team.

Small Team Meeting #2:

RESONATE AND REMIND AGENDA

1. Welcome everyone and open with some personal insights from your own experience in this process.

2. Start by focusing on the organizational core values that have been identified. The goal of this Small Team Meeting is to make the connection between personal and organizational core values. Just present the organizational values and avoid a wordsmith working session. That is already being addressed in the "refining" process!

3. Take each organizational core value (one at a time) and ask participants to share which of their personal values apply (for example, what personal core values do they employ each day to bring this specific organizational core value to life?).

4. Take each organizational core value and ask participants to share examples of positive behavior and negative behavior they have experienced in the daily environment (both what they do and what they see).

5. From the discussion above, have each participant think of three specific actions they can take to engage a specific personal core value that will support a related organizational core value.

6. Let the group know when the next Large Group Session will take place.

Follow-up assignment: Each participant will take their handout of committed actions and document examples of where, over the next couple of months, they have lived out that commitment. This will help build stories for the next meeting.

Facilitator Note: Remember, it is important to try to draw each person into the conversation so that all participants are engaged in the discussion. It is often helpful to sequentially go around the table for input or to randomly call on individuals while being sure you have called on everyone.

Emphasis and Challenges

In some ways, this may be one of the most difficult phases of all. It's been a number of months since you drew a line in the sand and started this journey. While hopefully the majority has had a great experience, most are still accustomed to high rates of change and flavor of the month initiatives coming on with great fanfare and then, just as quickly, fading away. As this prior experience of rapid organizational change combines with a greater number of personal and organizational standards of accountability, some folks might begin to hope it will just fade away. This phase might be considered "values fatigue."

This phase might be considered "values fatigue."

Not only will all of your people start getting values fatigue, *so will you.* You have been at it a lot longer than they have. You have to remain intentional even when you cognitively and even emotionally get tired of thinking about it. It won't be easy. This is why your personal commitment is so critical before you ever begin.

This is the most vulnerable stage you have to push through—somewhere in the six- to nine-month time frame of your journey. Like in most transitions, this window of time becomes the hardest. The current is starting to change directions, causing a lot of turbulence, but the flow is not yet reversed. When reversing the flow, there is a moment of transition where the flow isn't moving in either direction. It feels like everything is standing still.

If "values fatigue" were the only characteristic of this phase, that would be challenge enough. But the disappointments and back steps will prove to be the toughest. Some of those disappointments will be in regard to others. The worst will be in regard to yourself. This is not an easy process. It is not about perfection. That won't happen. It is about patience and persistence. Beginning with you.

The cadence of this process goes forward, and then it goes back and forth. You will see the trajectory gradually starting to move more consistently in the right direction. In the meantime, your day-to-day emotions will feel more like a yo-yo going up and down, back and forth, and all around. But relax; it's simply a case of normal.

It's in this phase that you are most vulnerable in wondering if your efforts were worth it. You start to fall into the trap of conventional wisdom, thinking *humans will just be human.* You will likely want to just get back to "normal" and forget about a new "normal," and so would most everyone else.

But values fatigue lends itself to recommitment. Recommitment is nurtured by the awareness of stories. We often experience failure because we give up just one step short of enormous success. This is the territory you're walking through when you're in the middle of *Resonate and Remind.*

Let's back up. Remember your journal? You need to continue filling the pages with all that you notice, documenting examples and stories. Except this time, it's not your stories. It's the stories you see all around you every day. Some will be simple stories, and others will be profound.

These are the stories of the value of values coming to life. These will become increasingly easy for you to see and necessary for you to communicate. In this phase, you have the opportunity and the necessity to become a student of your organizational core values, while teaching others to do the same. This phase is hard because of values fatigue. But it's also where you and those around you are most likely to turn the corner and begin to see the Return On Integrity.

11

Reinforce and Reenergize

Reaching the point of no return is indeed a critical
turning point in establishing the way forward.

Your *Prequel* experience, *Reset and Reboot, Reveal and Refine,* along with *Resonate and Remind,* were all phases designed to build a foundation, gain traction, and eventually build momentum. This final phase, *Reinforce and Reenergize,* is about making it all a way of life—the way forward.

Up to this point, it's been important to get individuals to own their part of the process, starting with their individual core values and then intersecting those values with the values of the organization. Nothing will build a stronger foundation for building a Return On Integrity than this personal ownership. The concepts pertaining to engaging your personal Drift Catchers and committing to your own PM/AM Examination are critical when it comes to personally reinforcing the process and keeping each individual reenergized.

In this phase, the emphasis shifts to everyone owning the whole process. While you still lead, this is about inspiring everyone else to own it all. Engaging the creativity and involvement of everyone is key to being able to *Reinforce and Reenergize.*

One way to build this ownership is through the Ambassadors facilitating Small Team Meeting #3. Another is by creating an incredible experience in your Large Group Session #4 to celebrate the success to date. Again, stories can make a significant and meaningful impact in bringing both emotional and intellectual aspects of the value of values to life. Stories should remain a key element in this final Large Group Session.

But it won't be enough.

There is another process, all too familiar, that will be needed as well. It's called measurement! Now that you're well into the process, everyone has had time to gain personal traction and momentum. It's time to evaluate the flow of things.

This measurement is subjective and is more focused on personal development than organizational judgment. In fact, you might think about it in terms of evaluating the health of personal and organizational integrity. It's called *Vital Signs.*

You might consider it more as taking your temperature. When we take the temperature of our body, the temperature is only one indicator of health. If you were to take your own temperature and notice a reading of 102 degrees, you would know that the temperature itself is not the problem, but rather is an indication that there is a problem. So too is the case with *Vital Signs.*

I don't believe you can measure core values per se, but you can take the temperature of the collective perception of the direction and strength of the flow of the river.

Vital Signs is intentionally designed to keep the focus on self and the inclusion of self when evaluating the broader organization. It's to encourage self-awareness rather than judgment of others. It also helps bring forth a focus and a better understanding of the expression of values through behaviors. This is done through not only asking for numerical evaluations of organizational core values but also looking for evidence that supports the evaluation. This evidence is expressed in terms of observed behaviors that either reinforce a specific value or diminish it.

This ever-building database of evidence creates a treasure of teachable moment materials for future understanding and further development of each organizational value.

A sample *Vital Signs* format is included on the following pages. You will see four sections:

- A self-evaluation on living one's own personal core values
- A self-evaluation on living each organizational core value
- An evaluation on how the organization (including self) is living each organizational core value
- Self-commitment

The *Vital Signs* tool is designed to be used every nine months. The timing is intentional in two ways:

- The nine-month cycle allows you to take the temperature continually at varying times of the year (different seasons of the calendar year and fiscal year). This prevents bias in the timing a certain month or business cycle might bring.
- It provides for a significant (but not too lengthy) amount of time to pass between taking each temperature. Core values is a long-term proposition, not a short-term measuring stick.

The *Vital Signs* concept is introduced in Small Team Meeting #3 by the Ambassadors and then administered at the completion of that series of Small Team Meetings and before your Large Group Session #4.

It's important the feedback is genuine and honest. A high level of confidentiality will be important. A simple online survey mechanism (e.g., SurveyMonkey) would be ideal. Having the results collected by a third

Sample Core Values Vital Signs Developmental Tool

1. Indicate YOUR perception that YOUR PERSONAL VALUES are being reflected in YOUR behaviors, decisions and relationships at work (FROM Very Strongly Agree = 10 TO Very Strongly Disagree = 1)

10	9	8	7	6	5	4	3	2	1
○	○	○	○	○	○	○	○	○	○

2. Indicate YOUR perception that OUR ORGANIZATIONAL VALUES are being reflected in YOUR behaviors, decisions and relationships at work (FROM Very Strongly Agree = 10 TO Very Strongly Disagree = 1)

	10	9	8	7	6	5	4	3	2	1
Organizational Value #1	○	○	○	○	○	○	○	○	○	○
Organizational Value #2	○	○	○	○	○	○	○	○	○	○
Organizational Value #3	○	○	○	○	○	○	○	○	○	○
Organizational Value #4	○	○	○	○	○	○	○	○	○	○
Organizational Value #5	○	○	○	○	○	○	○	○	○	○

3. Indicate YOUR perception that ORGANIZATIONAL VALUE #1 is being reflected in OUR ORGANIZATION'S behaviors, decisions and relationships (FROM Very Strongly Agree = 10 TO Very Strongly Disagree = 1)

10	9	8	7	6	5	4	3	2	1
○	○	○	○	○	○	○	○	○	○

Evidence (example of where you have seen this)

4. Indicate YOUR perception that ORGANIZATIONAL VALUE #2 is being reflected in OUR ORGANIZATION'S behaviors, decisions and relationships (FROM Very Strongly Agree = 10 TO Very Strongly Disagree = 1)

10	9	8	7	6	5	4	3	2	1
○	○	○	○	○	○	○	○	○	○

Evidence (example of where you have seen this)

5. Indicate YOUR perception that ORGANIZATIONAL VALUE #3 is being reflected in OUR ORGANI-ZATION'S behaviors, decisions and relationships at work (FROM Very Strongly Agree = 10 TO Very Strongly Disagree = 1)

10	9	8	7	6	5	4	3	2	1
○	○	○	○	○	○	○	○	○	○

Evidence (example of where you have seen this)

6. Indicate YOUR perception that ORGANIZATIONAL VALUE #4 is being reflected in OUR ORGANIZA-TION'S behaviors, decisions and relationships at work (FROM Very Strongly Agree = 10 TO Very Strongly Disagree = 1)

10	9	8	7	6	5	4	3	2	1
○	○	○	○	○	○	○	○	○	○

Evidence (example of where you have seen this)

7. Indicate YOUR perception that ORGANIZATIONAL VALUE #5 is being reflected in OUR ORGANI-ZATION'S behaviors, decisions and relationships at work (FROM Very Strongly Agree = 10 TO Very Strongly Disagree = 1)

10	9	8	7	6	5	4	3	2	1
○	○	○	○	○	○	○	○	○	○

Evidence (example of where you have seen this)

8. Based on my self-awareness in completing this Values Vital Signs Tool, I commit to the following action(s) to further align my behaviors, decisions and relationships with our organizational core values:

9. I have consistently lived the commitment I stated on my last Values Vital Signs Tool, (FROM Very Strongly Agree = 10 TO Very Strongly Disagree =1) Please write N/A only if this is your FIRST TIME taking the Values Vital Signs Tool.

10	9	8	7	6	5	4	3	2	1
○	○	○	○	○	○	○	○	○	○

Note: Actual organizational values are inserted in survey instead of Organizational Values #1–#5 party or someone at arm's length will go a long way in getting a more accurate reading on the temperature.

You are now positioned to move into this fourth phase of *Reinforce and Reenergize*.

Preparation

As before, the preparation for this phase will look familiar in structure but different in context. Everything in this phase is about positioning for the long-term sustainability of building Return On Integrity. The familiarity of the format should allow you to put all of your focus and energy into the content.

- Preparing Ambassadors to lead Small Team Meetings
- Administering the *Vital Signs* tool
- Preparing for Large Group Session #4

While the focus of the *Resonate and Remind* phase was about crossing the bridge from identification to application, the focus of this phase is preparing everyone to continually look inside, look around, and, most importantly, look across the horizon with an emphasis on long-term sustainability of increasing the potential of a rich Return On Integrity.

With the fourth and final Large Group Session, a key element of this phase is also setting into motion various creative ideas that keep core values front and center day to day. You now have an entire organization following you along this journey with both great insight and experience with the process. It's now time for everyone to get creative in thinking of fun, meaningful, specific, and tangible ways to permanently weave the commitment to personal and organizational core values into every aspect of the business infrastructure and daily operations.

The Ambassadors are in a great position to brainstorm numerous ideas in their Small Team Meetings. Large Group Session #4 is a great way to showcase some innovative ideas and announce their implementation. There is a lot of ground to cover in this final formal phase of *Reinforce and Reenergize*. It needs to be executed with a lot of energy.

[Preparing the Ambassadors]

By this point the Ambassadors should be very familiar with the process and with their Small Teams. As before, this is a good time to get a reading through the eyes of the Ambassadors on what they are seeing and hearing among their team and within their natural work setting.

It's also a great time to prepare them for their next Small Team Meeting by not only walking through the planned agenda but also living the agenda when it comes to collecting stories, brainstorming specific ideas for the long term, and walking through the *Vital Signs* tool and plans for its implementation. This will equip the Ambassadors with experience and specific examples to carry into their own meetings.

[Preparing for Large Group Session #4]

More than any other Large Group Session, this one should feel like a real celebration. There are a lot of ways you could approach this and a lot of ways to get others involved. Be sure to take the handcuffs off creativity and have some fun with this one. There are numerous elements of experiences you might consider:

- Celebrate the concept of story by having individuals effectively share expressions of a certain organizational core value through an impactful story to create various teachable moments.
- Create a well-produced video montage of numerous stories that reinforce various organizational core values. With the advancement of technology, you can easily produce a high-quality video experience on a low-cost budget.

- Have some of the Small Teams create fun skits that bring the organizational core values to life.

- Seek out the hidden talents of your people that might provide unique experiences to celebrate this journey of building a Return On Integrity. It might be a poet to create a poem, or a group of musicians to play a song. Quality is key here, but you might be surprised at the caliber of the hidden talent that walks your hallways each day.

- Prepare to share the results of your first *Vital Signs* survey. This creates a perfect opportunity to be genuine and authentic in sharing that building a Return On Integrity is an imperfect path of ever-increasing value. Give some observations on the results and explain how the *Vital Signs* will be used going forward.

- With a solid foundation in place, it's time to begin the conversation on how the commitment to personal and organizational core values will have a systemic impact on all aspects of the organization. This will be an ever-evolving process, but the following might be opportunities to make it tangible:

  ○ A revision of performance reviews and how organizational core values become an influential fabric of the evaluation process

  ○ The incorporation of communication and assessment of the organizational core values into the interview for hiring process

  ○ A review of all metrics and measurements for adherence to and encouragement of the organizational values as well as an evaluation of any unintended consequences of those ongoing measurement tools

  ○ An investigation into how current training and other development programs systemically enhance the organizational core values and where new programs could be developed to eliminate any voids that exist

○ A revision of the on-boarding process to incorporate a process that reflects the spirit of the four phases every current employee has just completed

It is in this long-term process that HR, marketing, and technology professionals can bring great value. Make sure you engage them in every aspect of the long-term horizon.

Consider having your Large Group Session #4 at the end of the day, where you have the opportunity to flow it into a post-meeting reception that carries on the theme of celebration. Be creative in how you can bring the *Return On Integrity* theme alive throughout the reception.

Gatherings

Just as in the prior phase, you have three gatherings ahead:

- Planning meeting with the Ambassadors
- Ambassadors' meetings with their Small Teams
- Everyone gathering for the fourth and final Large Group Session

We have thoroughly covered all you need to do for the Ambassador Meeting and the Large Group Session. The following Small Team Meeting #3 agenda should provide the details each Ambassador will need to prepare for facilitating their Small Team.

Small Team Meeting #3:

REINFORCE AND REENERGIZE

This final Small Team Meeting will address three areas: (1) sharing examples, through stories, of where the organizational core values are lived, (2) brainstorming ideas that keep core values front and center moving forward, and (3) explaining the upcoming use of the *Vital Signs* tool.

1. Welcome everyone and open with some personal insights on your own experience in this process.

2. Ask a few of the participants to share a specific story/example of one of the organizational core values in action. Share a solid example yourself . . . possibly even a couple of stories/examples to get things moving. Position these stories as sharing specific behaviors/decisions they have observed as opposed to self-reporting on their own behaviors/decisions. Listen carefully to their stories/examples and then "in the moment" relate how one of those stories is a "teachable moment" for you . . . reminding you how you can best live a specific value in one of your own upcoming meetings, decisions, or challenges. This models taking what others see and introspectively using it as your own developmental opportunity. Make note of specific stories that might be shared in Large Group Session #4 presented "live" by the individual sharing the story or through a possible video montage of stories.

3. Next, have each participant brainstorm ideas for keeping the organizational core values front and center going forward. This builds off the brainstorm initiated in the prior Large Group Session. Participants should bring the list of notes they started in that session as

well as the ideas they have brainstormed since then. Let them know that the Small Team leaders will compile the collective lists of all teams to discuss steps going forward.

4. Finally, discuss the upcoming *Vital Signs* assessment tool as one of the means of understanding the perception of how the core values are being lived (personally and organizationally). This instrument (ideally completed every nine months) will give a current reading as well as, over time, a trend analysis. It also gives a chance to begin to document example behaviors that reflect the values in action. It is important to remind everyone that only the cumulative data will be available to anyone at your organization and that the individual responses will remain confidential. Let the group know when the next Large Group Session will take place.

Facilitator Note: Remember, it is important to try to draw each person into the conversation so all participants are engaged in the discussion. It is often helpful to sequentially go around the table for input or to randomly call on individuals while being sure you have called on everyone.

Emphasis and Challenges

Once you cross the bridge from identification to application, the *Reinforce and Reenergize* phase should bring a feeling of confidence and celebration. You are over the hump and should be experiencing a new sense of momentum.

It's important to ignite that momentum in a fun way, to enjoy the moment and to build upon it as you look across the horizon. This phase moves from a launching process to simply a way of life.

This entire process has been about changing the direction of the flow of the river. Once the flow is reversed, you might wonder how there could be any challenges remaining.

The whole reason the engineers needed to reverse the flow of the Chicago River was because pollutants were being introduced into the river, which was subsequently flowing into Lake Michigan, the source of the community's drinking water. Once the flow was reversed, there was still the problem of pollutants in the river.

No matter how effectively you execute each phase of this process, you will still have pollutants being introduced into the flow. We're not talking about pollutants from the occasional drifts of those committed to living their personal and organizational core values. You have an organizational culture and individual accountability tools and habits that will help keep that in check.

The problem is the flagrant polluters. And they will become more evident than ever, more lethal in their systemic impact. It takes only a handful to destroy the credibility of all the work you have done. Depending on their position, sometimes it only takes one.

> **What destroys the process is not what they do—it's what you don't do.**

What destroys the process is not what they do—it's what you don't do. It is in this phase that it must be made clear: This is not a program or an initiative. This isn't going away. It's not to be something you can wait out and then return to operating however you wish. It is a defined way of life.

You've provided adequate training, encouragement, and support. And now you need to make it clear that an unwillingness to embrace a commitment to living identified personal core values and the stated values of the organization will have consequences.

By now, the current violators should be standing out like an infection. You can't afford to retain the infection in the system for very long. Yes, you can treat it with specific and fair warning. But you have about a ninety-day window to either cure the infection or amputate that part from the culture. This holds true regardless of the past or present performance of the violators.

Nothing will destroy your accomplishments and credibility faster than allowing an infection to go untreated.

When you are trying to establish and increase your Return On Integrity, you must note that integrity doesn't come in different degrees like sunscreen lotion. You are either committed to it or you are not. The time has come for each employee, manager, and executive to decide if they are ALL IN or they are OUT. If they can't seem to make that decision, you will have to make it for them. It is the responsibility and duty of leading.

> The time has come for each employee, manager, and executive to decide if they are ALL IN or they are OUT. If they can't seem to make that decision, you will have to make it for them. It is the responsibility and duty of leading.

12

The Call of Every Leader

Leadership is going to be about what you do . . .
but, first and foremost, about who you are.

So, are leaders born or made? I'm not sure we will ever know with certainty. I am certain that leadership is born at the core of any leader.

Leadership's greatest demand is simply a calling—a calling to your core. It doesn't care what you want to be in title. It has no regard for what you want to have in terms of things, status, or wealth. It asks only one question of you: Who are you?

When our focus is immersed totally in the *what*, the what will eventually change you. It's just a matter of time. It sneaks up on you, or more truthfully, you drift up on it.

Your core is who you are. It doesn't need a title to define status; it has the ability to show up in any role, at any time, on any day. The value in your core is just as valuable in any employee, whether they are a janitor, cashier, construction worker, doctor, or chief

> **Who are you?**
> **Your core is**
> **who you are.**

executive officer. Core values don't change in value because of context. They convey value to any context you bring them to.

Core values don't come in quantities—they either are or they aren't. Take any core value. Would you want just a little of it or a lot of it? It doesn't make sense in terms of quantity. Any of it is exactly the same as all of it. A value isn't defined by wealth, because it is already rich within itself. Whatever core value you name doesn't need to be the leader. That is not what this is about. *Return On Integrity* is about a leader *needing them.* And it starts with a genuine desire to search, discover, understand, embrace, and then endlessly live them. It's also important to understand they don't hold on to you. We must consciously hold on to them. If we don't, we drift. In the end, values don't need leadership. It just so happens, the quality of your leadership has everything to do with needing them.

> **Changing the flow of your own river is a choice. It's going to take a decision. Changing the flow of your organization is going to take everything you've got.**

Changing the flow of your own river is a choice. It's going to take a decision. Changing the flow of your organization is going to take everything you've got.

Critical Characteristics

In the two decades I have focused and spoken on leadership, there have been three common characteristics I have noticed in leaders of substance: *courage, vulnerability, and humility.*

In most cases, building a Return On Integrity is going to require reversing the flow, and reversing the flow is going to take great measures of courage, vulnerability, and humility.

[Courage]

It's tough to bring credibility to what most executives would consider to be a soft topic. And you can make yourself a soft target in trying to do so. This is especially true when the soft is really hard to do.

It takes courage. It especially takes courage when you are trying to understand it and create it as you build it. Any grand mission or vision comes with inherent risk. Especially when that mission is about who we are going to become rather than what we are going to do!

It also takes courage when the substance of progress isn't seen immediately or can't be measured directly by hard data. It also takes courage because the progress isn't consistent, sequential, or objective. It comes in spurts and sometimes in sudden, exponential bursts. The progress doesn't come in fiscal quarters; it comes in defining moments. It's not what we've become used to. It's likely not what you are used to either.

Courage replaces your need for continual reinforcement. It cushions the blows of those who will doubt you. It protects you from yourself on the days you doubt yourself. There will be days like these. Many days. Maybe every day.

The word "courage" comes from the Latin root word "*cor*," meaning "heart." That's why you have to find your personal commitment before you ever begin. It's from that commitment that you will find the courage you need and be able to continue to nurture that courage that you will ultimately draw upon to sustain yourself.

[Vulnerability]

Courage will give you the ability to be vulnerable, because vulnerability comes from a place of strength.

Weak leaders are the least likely to choose vulnerability because deep down, they already sense the vulnerability that stems from their weakness. Theirs is not a vulnerability they choose; it's a vulnerability they experience from a sense of weakness. You will often see this in followers who are in a position of leadership. When leaders hide their vulnerability, they encourage their followers to do the same. Leaders need to remember that followers do a great job—of following!

Strong leaders, on the other hand, *choose* vulnerability. It is a paradoxical strength they embrace.

> D———▶
> ## Strong leaders choose vulnerability. It is a paradoxical strength they embrace.

No one wants a weak leader. And I think we long for a leader strong enough and courageous enough to be willing to be vulnerable. Ironically, strong leaders who are willing to be vulnerable will eventually expose weak leaders without any effort of their own.

For twenty years, I have embraced vulnerability as one of the most defining characteristics of a great leader. It's probably why I became an early fan of the great work that PhD Brené Brown brought to light over this past decade. Like her, her work is incredibly refreshing, delightful—and vulnerable.

I'm convinced that a leader who doesn't embrace vulnerability will never experience a real Return On Integrity. They certainly will never lead one. Integrity is only found in our core, and our core is only discovered with the gift of vulnerability.

> D———▶
> ## Integrity is only found in our core, and our core is only discovered with the gift of vulnerability.

The inability to choose to be vulnerable creates the need to "spin." In many cases, the spin becomes more important than the truth, especially when we begin to believe our own spin as the truth. Leaders intentionally operating from their personal core and leading from the organization's core have nothing to spin. They realize vulnerability is a refreshing reality of life, and of leadership.

[Humility]

Vulnerability is born from courage, and both are nourished by humility.

Remember, values don't care about your title or position. They only care about who you are. It's easy to be humble when you are connected to them. It's much harder when you are grasping for or attached to a title or position.

This process is not about you; *it's about you leading a Return On Integrity*. And this difference is a subtly nuanced one. There is great freedom in realizing that difference.

It would seem a process that begins with you doing something as personal as connecting with your core would somehow have to be about you. But it's not. It's not about your position of leadership. Positions of leadership can become convenient attachments; so can ego. Humility releases you from these attachments by slowly loosening your grip so you can embrace courage and vulnerability.

Courage, vulnerability, and humility are dependable life preservers when you are going against the tide trying to reverse the flow.

The Irony of Soft

In the spirit of full disclosure, some executives may want to hold on to an image of core values as the soft stuff. Doing so will save them from a personally and organizationally demanding adventure, and their most demanding call as a leader. But it won't save them from a disaster waiting to happen. It will enable them to hold an executive position and the rewards that come with it without bearing the full weight of the demands of leadership. It will allow them to dodge the tough calls and hard decisions. It may save them from the experience of truly leading at all. Taking the "soft" route makes some things easier along the way—until you turn around at the end of your leadership journey and see what you missed.

Having to face what you failed to create can be very hard. Especially when it is too late.

Force Field Analysis

During my very young years, I loved the rides of amusement parks. I especially loved the ones that would spin and wreak havoc with your equilibrium. Two of my favorites were the Twister and the Scrambler. Unfortunately, as you get older, you have those moments when you experience the same sensation those rides provided—without ever going on the ride! It was fun to be spun around on those rides before life actually started doing it for you!

I find this to be the case for a lot of leaders. There is a lot of swirling around in their world. The relentless demands don't only make their head spin, they have the potential to create a gravitational pull.

Another amusement ride I found fascinating was simple in design. Everyone entered a large round room and stood on the floor with your back to the wall and your face to the center of the room. This room turned out to be a large spinning cylinder. It started spinning very slowly, but then started picking up speed at an ever-increasing rate. As the spinning cylinder reached top speeds, the floor slowly started dropping out from under your feet, ending up eight feet below you. You didn't drop at all, of course, because the force of the spinning cylinder held you firmly in place with your back against the wall. While the reason for what you were experiencing was obvious—it was also invisible.

A force field was at play.

I hadn't thought about that ride in years, until a very different kind of force field reminded me of it. Recently, I was tucked away at a very secluded writers' venue in Virginia working on the manuscript for this book.

For well over a decade, I've observed talented professionals, from various walks of life, seriously struggling to grasp the essence of the concept of core values. They have felt exasperation at various levels about trying to come to grips with the specifics of their own personal core values. These frustrations surfaced in an array of settings. Sometimes, while grasping for answers, they ended up asking me ever more clarifying questions. Individuals struggle with trying to name something that cognitively seems easy to name, while finding that this something remains elusive and invisible.

On that amusement ride, a force field held our bodies against the wall of the spinning cylinder as the floor slipped away. The nature of our lives, with their ever-increasing speed, can create their own force field as our core (when left unidentified) slips away from us—or more truthfully, as we drift away from it. Whichever way you want to look at it—the two (we and our core) aren't together as we should be. On that amusement ride, you would've had to break through the gravitational pull of the speed to jump to the sunken floor below.

Force fields can be tough to break through.

It's become clear to me that the struggle for an individual to name, understand, and embrace their core is not a cognitive issue. No matter how many clarifying questions regarding the nature of core values get answered, there will likely be more questions, frustration, and confusion. That is, until the invisible force field is penetrated.

It was the force field that I encountered at this secluded writers' venue in Virginia. It wasn't visible. You couldn't touch it or hug it, but you could certainly feel it. While you couldn't hear it, in so many ways, it was so loud it was impossible to ignore. It's not that I hadn't experienced it before. In fact, we all experience bits of it at some point every day. But not to the depth or length I experienced it in Virginia. It was the force field I had to penetrate to experience a breakthrough in my writing. It was uncomfortable and at times almost unbearable. I have personally watched a group of successful health-care executives unable to endure even a ten-minute prescription of it. It's called *silence*.

I'm not talking about an hour of silence followed by a discussion with others about the experience. I'm talking about hours building into days of complete silence with no one around to debrief about it. In the case of the health-care executives, some only made it ninety seconds after being instructed to sit in complete silence and ponder a specific question for just ten minutes. Most found the need to end the silence with the majority of the minutes remaining. The problem is that you can never understand what you leave prematurely.

At my writers' venue, there was no way to end that silence. I suppose I could have run from it, which I actually considered for a moment, but I couldn't end it. Unlike penetrating the gravitational field of the spinning cylinder of that amusement ride, silence isn't something you muster a force of energy to push through.

Silence is something you surrender to.

In the midst of your surrender to silence, you begin to hear again. You begin to see again. It's with increasing clarity that you begin to hear and see the invisible—the thoughts that sit within your core.

While it may sound simple, it was a huge revelation to me as to why it's been so difficult for smart, successful professionals to make an authentic connection to their core. A mile-long list of answered questions will never add up to the clarity that days of deafening silence will reveal. I suppose, in years gone past, there were wonderful sessions of silence experienced on many a front porch!

I believe I've only scratched the surface. It's a surface I will continue to ponder—*in more silence*. You might ask what leader can afford to take a few days away to go into a complete seclusion of uninterrupted silence. Maybe the better question may prove to be, what leader can afford not to? Maybe this is why so many people don't know the specifics of the values at their own core or the core of the organizations in which they spend most of their waking hours.

As I left Virginia, I concluded that if I were on the board of directors of a public company, I would require our CEO to go away each year for one week to a venue of complete silence. No strategy, vision, mission documentation, or books of board minutes; just a list of their personal core values and our organization's core values—*and the opportunity for nothing but silence.* I am convinced after that week, that CEO would be exponentially more effective throughout the other fifty-one weeks of the year.

Don't Go It Alone

Going it alone is a bad idea. That's precisely why you need the commitment (not support) of those around you. While this would include those with governing responsibilities (such as a board of directors or joint-venture capitalists) in organizations financially governed or owned by others, it also includes those around you, members of your leadership team, HR, marketing, and technology. Of course, you don't want or need their commitment until you are certain you have found your own.

While these are important individuals to have alongside you, these are not the people I'm referring to when I suggest you not go it alone. I'm talking about other CEOs and owners who have found the same personal and organizational commitment as you have.

You will need one another along the way. They will serve as impactful confidants. They will prove a great source of nourishment for your courage, vulnerability, and humility. They will be a resourceful pool of best practice ideas that stimulate creativity and progress along the way. And you will be just the same to them.

Most importantly, they will understand your journey like no one else.

Linchpin Leadership

There is one thing you, alone, do hold: *the role to lead this.* You are the linchpin in the entire process. While core values don't yearn for a title, never underestimate what your platform can do in bringing credibility, authenticity, and accountability to the process.

Where you go in this process, so goes the process. Don't sell your impact or influence short. The potential for negative or positive is all the same—significant. Also, don't underestimate the significant potential when the flow carries within it a commitment to personal and organizational core values.

Legacy

I think most leaders, at some point in their career, think about the legacy they might leave behind. Unfortunately, some think of it on the eve of their retirement party. They wonder what others will say about them. At that point, it's too late and is in the mouths of others.

How will I be remembered?

Core values are the most impactful and untapped resource any leader has at their disposal. They are also the seeds from which legacies are grown.

Most often when I hear leaders speak about their legacy well before their retirement party, I hear them pose the question *How will I be remembered?*

It's a logical question. I would suggest, however, that it is the wrong question.

Your legacy isn't about how you are remembered. It's about what you leave behind. The better legacy question would be this: *What am I going to do with what I've been given?*

What am I going to do with what I've been given?

I have never met an executive who hasn't been given a lot. Worked hard, yes, but has been given to abundantly. They might have been given opportunity, development, trust, a second chance . . . and on and on and on.

The question isn't asking if I have been given much. That is a given! The question is, "What am I going to do with what I've been given?"

This is one of the nice things about core values. They are only valuable if you give them away. They are designed to serve others. The nice thing about core values, as long as you stay connected to them, is they never run out. They keep replenishing themselves as long as you discover them and stay connected to your core.

You are the linchpin for leadership—core values are the linchpin for you.

> The question isn't asking if I have been given much. That is a given!

Closing Thoughts

Three years ago, on a mid-spring day, I sat on this very same rock bench in the beautiful Spruce Plot of the Morton Arboretum in Lisle, IL. By that time, I had focused on and taught a great deal about numerous aspects of leadership. As I sat on the bench, one thing had become clear to me: We can focus on leadership skills, organizational methodologies, programs, and productivity for as long as we want. We can do it over and over again. We can add updated terminology and new angles. But until we become crystal clear on core values and their fabric of integrity, it becomes impossible to truly lead—at least in the right direction.

In leadership, there is so much at stake. When an individual drifts, it can be devastating. When a leader drifts, it is likely to be catastrophic.

On that spring day, as I wrote the words that, still today, remain in the "Opening Thoughts" of this book, I was certain that by the following closing days of autumn, I would return to this same bench with a completed manuscript. I envisioned it capturing my thoughts, insights, and point of view in a book titled *Return On Integrity*. I had no idea it would be on the fifth day of spring—*three years later.*

I was focused on writing about the journey awaiting leaders. I had no idea of the nature of the journey awaiting me. I had no idea of the resistance, the distractions, the confusion, and most often the desire to want to give up along the way. Those were the roadblocks I found—inside of me.

I would eventually realize that each roadblock served a purpose in helping me experience microcosms of what I now believe every leader will encounter if they choose to build a real *ROI*:

- It takes longer than you can possibly conceive.
- It seems so simple and straightforward until it gets so very confusing.
- There is incredible resistance from within and from without.
- Other good things will distract you.
- What seems so straightforward can be so elusive.
- The end in mind can be distracting when there really isn't one.
- *Who* you are and *how* you get there are the same—letters in a different order.
- There is no efficiency, only effectiveness.
- Vision isn't about where you're headed—it's about how your values open your eyes.

*   *   *

Even as I write these closing words, I fight the urge to put the emphasis, the hope, and the reward on the *return* part of integrity. Because the *getting* in this return is *getting back* what you have *given* to integrity.

Integrity is the return. It is return enough. There is no glitz, false promises, or smoke and mirrors. The return is truth.

You can't take the truth to the bank, yet it's the only real value of your journey. It's what brings value to our relationships, our work, our passions, and ultimately our legacy.

Your Return On Integrity is not about what you value—it's about what your values ARE.

When I first sat on this rock bench, I had clarity about the idea of personal and organizational core values being the linchpin of leadership. But I wasn't prepared for how unclear my clarity would become when well-meaning conversations, challenging questions, and condescension parading as sophistication made me wonder if there was any merit in my simple idea at all.

> **Your Return On Integrity is not about what you value—it's about what your values ARE.**

I found it extremely difficult for people to stay focused on core values themselves. When they heard the phrase "core values," they wanted to translate it or to make it about something else. It made me realize how little we understand about the essence of core values or how much we cognitively diminish their strategic importance.

During the journey of these three years, I have shared the title of this book with countless people. Ninety-nine percent had the same physical reaction when they heard the title. This reaction played so repetitively that I began to notice it and eventually watch for it. As I would say *"Return On,"* you could sense the assumption and you could almost feel the programmed momentum of their mind as it headed to "Investment." Almost on cue, as I said *Integrity*, there was a mild form of whiplash as their eyebrows shot upward to the heavens and their heads jerked back a bit.

It was precisely these repeated moments that continued to encourage me and push me to take the next step forward.

Integrity may not be what we have come to expect at the end of *ROI*. But I do believe it's what each of us deeply desires from the beginning.

Nineteen years ago, as I began my journey in speaking and writing, I made a decision. I never wanted to be someone who claimed to have all the answers. I truly believe others have done this quite well, and have brought great value, wisdom, and insight into our marketplace. But that isn't me. It's never been my pursuit or purpose. I simply wanted to be someone who got smart people thinking more deeply, more genuinely, and more authentically about the deceptively simple essence of what mattered the most.

I had to remind myself of this a thousand times while writing this manuscript.

This book is not as much about getting it right, as it is about doing what is right; I trust that in doing what is right, you will certainly get more right in return.

My hope is that *Return On Integrity* furthers a conversation that's been taking place throughout the ages, sometimes in the foreground and sometimes in the background. There are times when the conversation fades away or gets pushed aside as irrelevant. When others push the conversation to the side, leaders rediscover it in the silence of their core. It's precisely where they reignite the conversation within themselves and eventually within their organization.

I have learned over these three years that I don't know all the twists and turns along this road. Sometimes I temporarily get lost. And you will too. Being lost is an important part of this journey of discovery.

I'm more convinced than ever that this path leads you in the right direction as you lead others. It is a path that leads you—and everyone else—to somewhere worthwhile, to a destiny defined by integrity.

As vague as it sometimes may seem, at some point you have to stop asking questions, stand up, and start walking.

In the Spruce Plot
At the Morton Arboretum
Lisle, Illinois

Love and truth form a great leader . . .
sound leadership is found in loving integrity.

Proverbs 20:28
—*The Message*

Acknowledgments

I often think of this book as the one-year project that took three years to complete. The real truth is that the work on this book began many years before I ever sensed a calling to write it.

It certainly began with a mom who loved me and showed me what integrity looked like—sometimes through words but mostly through actions. Etna Blumberg was my first Drift Catcher. There were also some incredible teachers—Sister Clare Marie, Pam Petersen, and Debbie Dunlap—who not only guided and inspired me but also believed in me. Their belief was more valuable than they will ever know.

My eighteen years at Arthur Andersen were priceless. The people of Arthur Andersen revealed for me what integrity looks like in the marketplace. The culture of the firm wasn't a brand; it was real and is why that connection still lives on—more than a decade beyond the implosion of the firm. The alumni of the firm will tell you they can't explain it, but they do experience it. Integrity does have a feeling. It is defined not by an organization but, rather, by those who collectively live in that organization. There are simply too many specific people to acknowledge by name.

I trust they know who they are, and as they read this, they know they are individually named in the depth of my heart with enormous gratitude.

At the same time, I would be remiss in a book written for leaders at the top not to acknowledge the incredible run of bosses that led me through those years at Andersen: Jerry West, Jim LaBorde, Jack Henry, and Denny Reigle were each an incredible blessing in their own unique way. I could write a chapter on each one of them and how each prepared me for this journey. They were each more than a boss. They were each a mentor and, ultimately, a friend. I think of them often and love each one of them.

Then there is Dave Houser. He never needed a title to be the boss. He stretched a lot of us to see much farther than most bother to look and to believe we could get there. We traveled the world together, teaching the Practice Management Leadership Workshop. In doing so, I watched Dave teach on core values more times than I can count or remember. I always paid attention rather than busying myself getting ready to teach the module on vision that was to follow. Little did I know, in the years ahead, that would prove to be a really good decision.

The people of Arthur Andersen also cheered me on as I made the decision to follow my dream into the world of professional speaking. And some incredible speakers were there to catch me when I jumped into it all. The first was Kevin Freiberg. He loved me from the beginning and held my hand through those early fragile years. Meeting Barbara Glanz was a blessing. We created a Mastermind Group that still exists today. Everyone who has been a part of each season of the evolution of that group has had an impact on my journey and my message. Joe Healey, Manny Garza, Eileen McDargh, and Emory Austin have each been inspiring members along the way. Today, Barbara Glanz, Jolene Brown, and Beverly Smallwood continue to guide me and challenge me each step of the way. They have walked the journey of this book project, hearing more than they probably ever wanted to know while still asking to hear more. There are not enough words to describe their friendship and their endless outpouring of encouragement. Naomi Rhode has been such a gift. Over many years, Naomi has been an incredible example of fully embracing the privilege of the platform and personally living everything this book is about. Most recently, she has been nothing short of a fresh gust of wind in my sails. Last but not least is Mark LeBlanc. As my business coach over the last fifteen years, he has been a refreshing mix of deep challenges, great discipline, incredible insights, and thoughtful listening. Like integrity, he has lovingly held me accountable.

Jimi Allen means everything to me. The public expression of what I do through website, photography, video, blog, and more are all amazing things he creates to equip me professionally. Yet, none of that compares to how he equips me personally. I will forever cherish our long discussions on the very content of this book and how it comes to life in our world.

The content of this book has been deepened by the tough questions and insights of Dave Sparkman, Roycee Kerr, Steve Blumberg, and Jason Passe. Thanks to them for holding me accountable to continually keep pulling out my own shovel when I was certain I had dug deep enough.

Neither this book nor my first book, *Silent Alarm*, would have seen the light of day without Clint Greenleaf. I can't imagine this journey without Clint and his genuine friendship. His brutal honesty makes me laugh, and the doors he invited me through allowed me to write.

The entire team at the Greenleaf Book Group is amazing. My thanks to Tanya Hall, for staying with me along this way. As CEO, she is always willing to answer the questions I should be asking someone else, yet always genuinely smiles and asks whether there is anything else. It has been a decade since Jay Hodges was my Greenleaf Book Group editor on *Silent Alarm*. It was great to reconnect with him as the Project Development Editor on *Return On Integrity*. He makes the editing process a true collaboration and learning experience. He took both projects to a level I could have never achieved without him. I was a bit nervous moving on to the next phase of editors without Jay, but Sally Garland, Elizabeth Brown, Marianne Tatom, and Tonya Trybula fully invested in taking our work to a further refined level. All of them showed incredible grace in their honest guidance. Nathan True and Neil Gonzalez both brought their creative gifts in evolving the reader's visual experience from cover to cover and everything in between. And Emilie Lyons, along with Carrie Jones, guided the ship, making sure it all came together! I so enjoyed working with each and every one of them. When I see the cover of the book, I see each of their names fully displayed along with mine.

The journey of writing a book can be a long and winding road. Like a marathon, you need people all along the way, cheering you on. Shawn Williams, Don Brooks, Sam Cole, Mary Jo Hazard, Al Gustafson, Andy Williames, Rob Arning, Jeff Mills, Brad Preber, Mark Blumberg, Philip Kreis, Sue Komarynsky, Jim Brown, Bob Hursthouse, Dr. Tom Nelson, Jeff and Janice Rubin, Tammy Young and my entire Ignatian Retreat Group, they haven't only cheered on this book and the message it contains; they have cheered me on for life. There are no words to express how much I love each and every one of them.

I also want to thank Trudy Hale for creating such a wonderful environment at The Porches Writing Retreat, in Norwood, Virginia. She gives two wonderful gifts to every writer who goes there: space and silence.

And finally, those I love the most: My wife and partner for life, Cindy, along with our three children, Ryan, Kelly, and Julie. I can't imagine life without them and am so grateful I don't have to. Just when I think I could never love them more, I do.

I'm sure I have forgotten to name even more than I remembered. Long after this book goes to print, they will cross my mind. I will cringe with my forgetfulness and then embrace my gratitude for them all the more.

To all of them, from the very depth of my core, I am forever grateful.

Index

About the Author

Simply put, John G. Blumberg is inspiring a movement among top executives to engage at the intersection of personal and organizational core values as the most impactful and untapped resource available to them as a leader.

In 1996, John left behind a career he loved—a career that had taken him from CPA to worldwide recruiting responsibilities at Arthur Andersen. From there, he followed his dream as a professional speaker to reach audiences in ten countries on three continents. John has received the designation of Certified Speaking Professional from the National Speakers Association, a designation held by less than 10 percent of the members of the International Federation of Professional Speakers.

Today, John walks alongside the top leaders of organizations who want to build their own Return On Integrity, as well as sharing his message on ROI to all who care to explore the depth of their own core. He is also the author of *Silent Alarm* (Greenleaf Book Group) and *GOOD to the CORE* (Simple Truths).

John lives in Naperville, Illinois, with his wife, Cindy, where they raised their three children, Ryan, Kelly, and Julie.